GO IN AND OUT THE WINDOW

AN ILLUSTRATED SONGBOOK
FOR YOUNG PEOPLE

MUSIC ARRANGED AND EDITED
BY
DAN FOX

COMMENTARY
BY
CLAUDE MARKS

THE METROPOLITAN MUSEUM OF ART
HENRY HOLT AND COMPANY
NEW YORK

Front cover and title page: Hand-tinted lithograph from L'An. *Franz M. Melchers, Belgian, 1868–1944. Brussels: E. Lyon-Claesen, 1897.*
Back cover: Snap the Whip *(detail). Winslow Homer, American, 1836–1910. Oil on canvas, 1872.*
Pages 3, 4, and 144: Illustrations from Vieilles chansons et rondes pour les petits enfants.
Maurice Boutet de Monvel, French, 1851–1913. Paris: Librairie Plon.

With the following exceptions, all works of art in this book were photographed by
The Metropolitan Museum of Art Photograph Studio: pages 22–23, Eric Pollitzer; page 39,
Bob Hanson; pages 117 and 126, Malcolm Varon; page 122, Paul Worchal.

Grateful acknowledgement is made to the following for permission to reproduce works of art:
Mark Baum; the Estate of Alexander Calder; Maurice Heaton; and Yvonne Jacquette.
Grandma Moses: *Thanksgiving Turkey,* copyright © 1987, Grandma Moses Properties Co.,
New York.

Published by The Metropolitan Museum of Art, New York, and Henry Holt and Company,
Inc., 115 West 18th Street, New York, New York 10011. Published in Canada by Fitzhenry &
Whiteside Limited, 195 Allstate Parkway, Markham, Ontario L3R 4T8.

Produced by the Department of Special Publications,
The Metropolitan Museum of Art
Type set by Advance Graphic, New York
Music engraved by W. R. Music Service, New York
Printed and bound by A. Mondadori, Verona, Italy
Designed by Miriam Berman

Library of Congress Cataloging-in-Publication Data:

Go in and out the window.

    Illustrations from the collections of The
Metropolitan Museum of Art.
    Includes index.
    Summary: An illustrated collection of sixty-one
traditional songs.
    1. Children's songs. [1. Songs] I. Fox, Dan.
II. Marks, Claude. III. Metropolitan Museum of Art
(New York, N.Y.)
M1997.G6 1987   87-752208
ISBN 0-87099-500-6 (MMA)
ISBN 0-8050-0628-1 (Henry Holt)

10 9 8 7 6 5

CONTENTS

PREFACE

Gathered together in this book are sixty-one songs of childhood—happy songs and sad songs, songs of work and songs of play, songs for young children and songs for older girls and boys. Some are about familiar birds and beasts, others about villages and cities that young people are likely to know or about the activities and trades with which they are most familiar. The diversity of the songs reflects the many different kinds of music that children have grown up with over hundreds of years.

Our selection is traditional rather than contemporary. We have chosen to exclude songs from popular radio or television programs and from movies or the theater. Because excellent songbooks featuring holiday music abound, we have left out songs celebrating Christmas and Hanukkah. What you will find are examples of each genre of childhood music: nursery songs, ballads, play songs, lullabies, folk songs, spirituals, and work songs, plus a sprinkling of patriotic music. The songs are presented alphabetically rather than by theme or type.

In arranging the music, the aim has been simplicity and clarity. All the selections are suitable for beginning to intermediate musicians and each is accompanied by guitar chords. A fingering chart for all the chords appears on page 144.

The images from The Metropolitan Museum of Art come from countries as culturally diverse as Japan, Mexico, England, and Egypt and span thousands of years. Each piece of art has been chosen to amplify the meaning of a song.

It is in the mixture of music and art that the magic of this book lies. The commentary that appears along with each song explores this magic, discussing the music, the art, and the combination of the two. It is our hope that this unique presentation will cause songs that have delighted many generations to be experienced afresh.

A NOTE ON THE GUITAR CHORDS

When the piano arrangement is in a key that is awkward for the guitar, capo instructions and alternate chords are given. After the capo is in place, the songs should be played using the chords that appear in parentheses.

ALL THE PRETTY LITTLE HORSES

This tender lullaby was very popular in the American South, hummed over cradles by parents and nurses. Some people count sheep when trying to fall asleep, but it is much more pleasant to think, and perhaps dream, of "pretty little horses" like the one in this print by the French artist Henri Matisse. He used brilliantly colored paper cutouts to create a joyous circus design with a bright pink horse and a coiling yellow line that suggests a ringmaster's whip.

Two Young Girls at the Piano (detail). Pierre Auguste Renoir, French, 1841–1919. Oil on canvas, 1892.

The Horse, the Rider, and the Clown. Henri Matisse, French, 1869–1954. Stencil-printed sheet from *Jazz*. Paris: Tériade, 1947.

Gently

Hush - a - bye, don't you cry, Go to sleep-y, lit-tle

ba - by. When you wake, you shall have

(Please turn the page.)

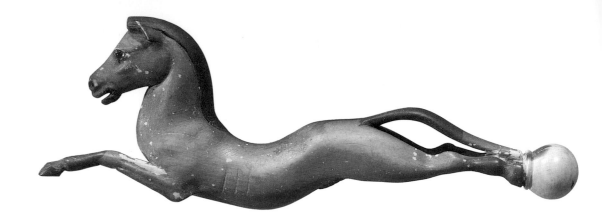

Egyptian craftsmen made even the smallest objects beautiful. This whip handle, shown almost actual size, is carved appropriately in the form of a prancing horse and is stained in reddish brown with a black mane. Both eyes once held garnets. The whip handle was made three hundred years after horses were introduced into Egypt from Asia. Horses became so popular that one Egyptian official had his Arabian horse buried, along with a pet monkey, near his own tomb. The horse was wrapped in linen still wearing its saddlecloth, then placed in a wooden casket to spend eternity close to his master.

ALL THE PRETTY LITTLE HORSES (Continued)

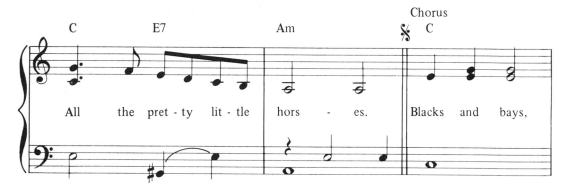

Whip handle. Egyptian (Thebes), Dynasty 18, ca. 1379–1362 B.C. Stained ivory with garnet.

*Last time, end here

8

Am   Dm

ba - by.   When you wake, you   shall have cake   And

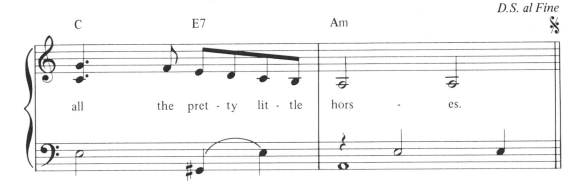

C   E7   Am   *D.S. al Fine*

all   the pret - ty lit - tle   hors -   es.

Inrō. Japanese, early 19th century. Red takamakie (raised design with gold) and mother-of-pearl.

This Japanese case is called an *inrō* and was used to store medicine. *Inrō* were once part of the costume of every fashionably dressed Japanese man, worn suspended from the waist by a cord. This one is only a few inches square and is made of wood almost as thin as paper. Over the wood the artist laid many coats of lacquer, a kind of varnish, allowing each coat to dry. He then drew the horses with powders of gold, silver, and other colors, making them into a lovely design raised above the red background. The little horse in mother-of-pearl catches the light in quite a delightful way.

Moderately

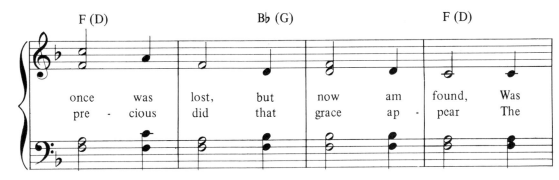

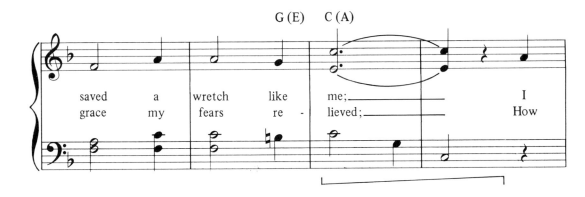

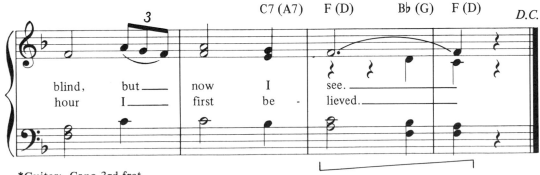

*Guitar: Capo 3rd fret

AMAZING GRACE

This hymn is about wonder, and that is what the French painter Paul Gauguin felt when he first came to the island of Tahiti in the South Seas. He had given up a career in business to be an artist, and he believed that people living in big cities could never become close to nature. In this far-away land, he hoped to find a life of joy and peace. Gauguin loved the lush colors of the tropical scenery and the beauty and grace of the Tahitians. Their old religion was dying out, so Gauguin painted a Christian subject, Mary and the Infant Jesus with an angel and two worshipers, as the Tahitians might have imagined them. This is unlike any other religious painting. Mary and one of the worshiping women wear flowered garments, the angel has yellow wings, there are bananas in the foreground, and the mountains and flowering trees, painted in purples and greens, create a mysterious, beautiful, and peaceful atmosphere.

Additional verses:

3.
Through many dangers, toils,
   and snares
I have already come;
'Tis grace hath brought me safe
   thus far
And grace will lead me home.

4.
Yea, when this flesh and heart
   shall fail
And mortal life shall cease;
I shall possess within the veil
A life of joy and peace.

Ia Orana Maria **(detail). Paul Gauguin, French, 1848–1903. Oil on canvas, 1891.**

11

The tune of "America" originated in England, and for well over two hundred years has been the tune of the British national anthem "God Save the King" or "God Save the Queen," as the case might be. The same melody inspired works in Danish, Dutch, German, and other languages. "Washington Crossing the Delaware," one of the most famous and popular paintings of a stirring episode in American history, is by the German-born artist Emanuel Leutze, and was painted in his Düsseldorf studio. His first picture was damaged by fire, so he painted a second version. An American visitor posed for the life-size figures of Washington and the man steering the main boat, and Leutze had an exact copy made of Washington's uniform. However, many details were invented by the artist to make the scene more dramatic. In reality, a heavier boat was used, the flag that whips in the wind was not adopted until six months later, and General Washington was seated, not standing, or he would have rocked the boat! But Leutze captures the spirit of the event, when on Christmas night in 1776, Washington and his men crossed the Delaware River, battling ice floes and a heavy snowstorm, and arrived at daybreak at Trenton. There they staged a surprise attack on the Hessian troops, leading to a victory that helped turn the tide of the American Revolution.

Washington Crossing the Delaware.
Emanuel Gottlieb Leutze, American, 1816–1868. Oil on canvas, 1851.

Slow and stately

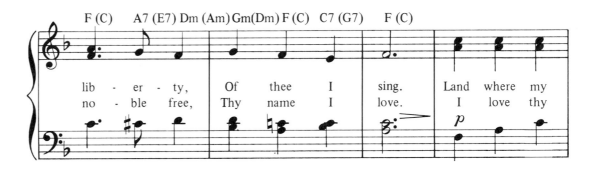
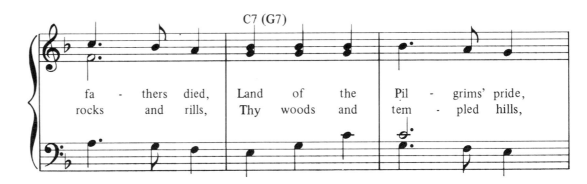
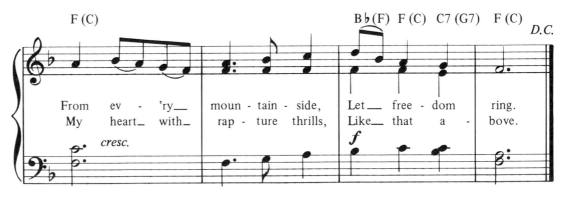

1. My coun - try, 'tis of thee, Sweet land of lib - er - ty, Of thee I sing. Land where my fa - thers died, Land of the Pil - grims' pride, From ev - 'ry___ moun - tain - side, Let___ free - dom ring.

2. My na - tive coun - try thee, Land of the no - ble free, Thy name I love. I love thy rocks and rills, Thy woods and tem - pled hills, My heart___ with___ rap - ture thrills, Like___ that a - bove.

AMERICA

*Guitar: Capo 5th fret

AMERICA THE BEAUTIFUL

Although it is not the national anthem, this song is very popular in the United States, for its noble sentiments and stately rhythms evoke the beauty, grandeur, and variety of the vast land set between two great oceans. Many American landscape painters in the last century recorded on canvas such imposing sights as Niagara Falls and the Grand Canyon. Thomas Moran, born in England and influenced by the famous English romantic landscapist J.M.W. Turner, joined several exploring expeditions to the Yellowstone and Rocky Mountain regions and became known as a leading painter of the American West.

Moran considered "The Teton Range," composed in his New York studio, to be his finest mountain landscape. It is not an accurate representation of any one view, but was painted from various studies and photographs that Moran made in Wyoming. The artist wanted to capture a mood, and he did so through the dramatic play of sunlight and shadow and by contrasting the large rock on the right with the majestic snow-covered mountains in the distance.

Eagle. American, 19th century. Gilded pine.

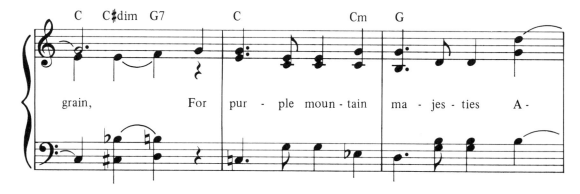

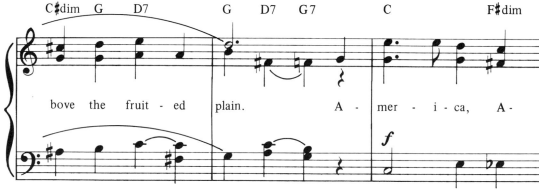

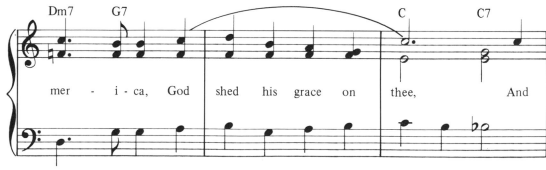

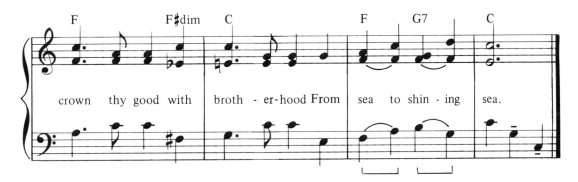

crown thy good with broth - er-hood From sea to shin - ing sea.

The Teton Range (detail). Thomas Moran, American, 1837–1926. Oil on canvas, 1897.

BAA, BAA, BLACK SHEEP

For more than two hundred years, "Baa, Baa, Black Sheep" has been a favorite nursery rhyme in Britain and America, but the tune may have come from France, where it is sung with different words. Some breeds of sheep yield more wool than others, and the black sheep in the song has enough for three people. Another version of the song, however, says that there will be "*none* for the little boy who *cries* in the lane," which seems most unfair!

In this stylized scene of country life from New England, there are three black sheep in the foreground. All the animals look as stiff as toys, even the hounds that are busy chasing a deer. In England and America, colored wool and silk were often embroidered on linen to make pictures like this one.

Detail of a needlework picture. Keturah Rawlins, American. Wool, silk, and metal threads on linen ground, ca. 1740.

Allegretto

Baa, baa, black sheep, have you an-y wool?

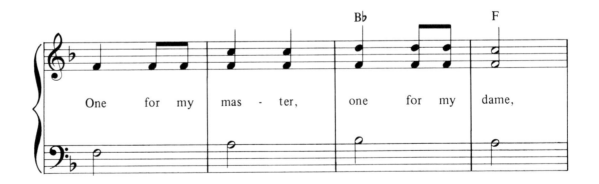

Yes, sir, yes, sir, three bags full.

One for my mas - ter, one for my dame,

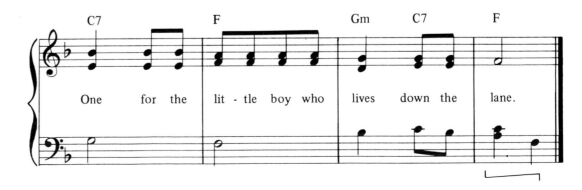

One for the lit - tle boy who lives down the lane.

As we now know it, this song is playful and teasing, but the tune and some of the words come from a much older English ballad, "Lord Randal." In it, Lord Randal dies after being poisoned by his lover. We can easily imagine "charming Billy" looking like the rosy-cheeked shepherd boy in François Boucher's painting, one of a series of four. Here he ties a love letter to the neck of the carrier pigeon perched on a ledge behind his knees as he points the way to his shepherdess-sweetheart's home. Boucher painted another picture with the messenger arriving, a third showing the sweetheart confiding the pigeon's message to a friend, and a final scene where the two lovers meet. We wonder whether Billy's courtship will have such a happy outcome. Although his love, "the darling" of his life, may be as pretty and dimpled as Boucher's shepherdess, and no doubt bakes a delicious cherry pie, her age, if the last verse is any clue, could be a problem, especially if at eighty-five she *still* cannot leave her mother!

BILLY BOY

The Dispatch of the Messenger.
**François Boucher, French, 1703–1770.
Oil on canvas, 1765.**

Not fast ($\downarrow$ = 1 beat)

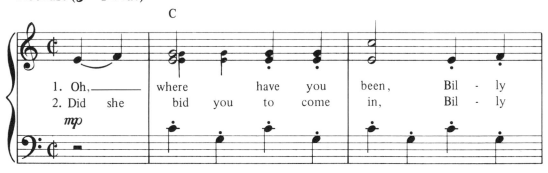

1. Oh,_____ where have you been, Bil - ly
2. Did she bid you to come in, Bil - ly

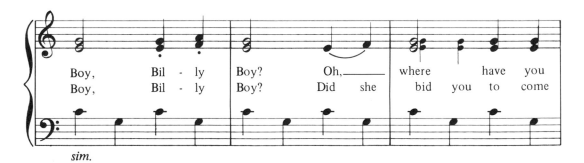

Boy, Bil - ly Boy? Oh,_____ where have you
Boy, Bil - ly Boy? Did she bid you to come

sim.

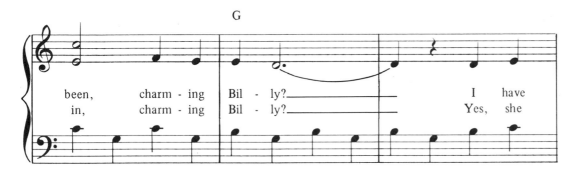

been,   charm - ing   Bil - ly?_____   I have
in,   charm - ing   Bil - ly?_____   Yes, she

Canning label. American, 19th century. Color lithograph.

been   to   seek   a   wife,   She's   the   dar - ling   of   my
bade   me   to   come   in,   There's   a   dim - ple   on   her

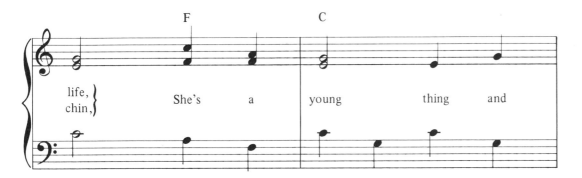

life,   She's   a   young   thing   and
chin,

Additional verses:

3.
Can she bake a cherry pie,
    Billy Boy, Billy Boy?
Can she bake a cherry pie,
    charming Billy?
She can bake a cherry pie
In the twinkling of an eye,
She's a young thing and
    cannot leave her mother.

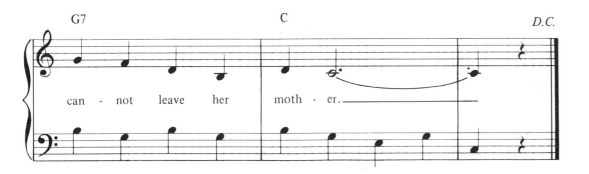

can - not   leave   her   moth - er._____   *D.C.*

4.
How old is she,
    Billy Boy, Billy Boy?
How old is she,
    charming Billy?
She's three times six,
    four times seven,
Twenty-eight and eleven,
She's a young thing and
    cannot leave her mother.

BINGO

If the intelligent-looking dog on the left had lived on an English or American farm, he might have been called Bingo like the dog in the song. But he belonged to a French viscount, who probably used him for hunting. He is a special breed of beagle, and was painted from life by Rosa Bonheur, famous in her day as a painter of animals at a time when there were very few professional women artists. In this small painting she tried to get an exact likeness of a handsome dog, whose alert expression and tense pose suggest that he may be following the scent of a trail.

Brightly (♩ = 1 beat)

There was a farm-er who had a dog, And Bing-o was his

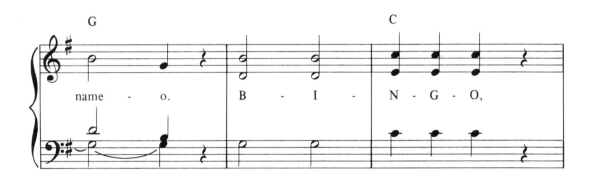

name - o. B - I - N - G - O,

B - I - N - G - O, B - I -

All Right! Nathaniel Currier, American, 1803–1887. Firm of Currier and Ives, active 1835–56. Hand-colored lithograph, ca. 1850.

A Limier Briquet Hound (detail). Rosa Bonheur, French, 1822–1899. Oil on canvas.

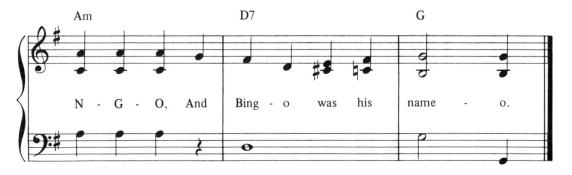

N - G - O, And Bing-o was his name - o.

21

The Harvesters (July)
(detail).
Pieter Bruegel the
Elder, Flemish,
active by 1551, d. 1569.
Oil on wood, 1565.

Many writers, poets, and artists have celebrated harvest time, when the ripened crops are gathered and country people can see the result of their hard work in the fields. No artist ever painted the harvest season more beautifully than the great Flemish master Pieter Bruegel the Elder. He captured the warm color of the wheat fields under a hazy sky on a hot summer's day as men and women harvest the grain, bind the sheaves, and carry them to a loaded wagon. The young man plodding along the path cut through the great golden mass of wheat carries jugs of drink to the weary workers eating their noonday meal under the splendid tree. One burly peasant has dozed off, his legs stretched out like the hands of a clock. Bruegel understood the life of the peasants, with its joys and hardships, and whether they are working or resting, each gesture is keenly observed. The more we look at this wonderful picture, the more there is to discover.

BRINGING IN THE SHEAVES

Moderately (♩ = 1 beat)

1. Sow - ing in the morn - ing, sow - ing seeds of kind - ness,
2. Sow - ing in the sun - shine, sow - ing in the sha - dows,

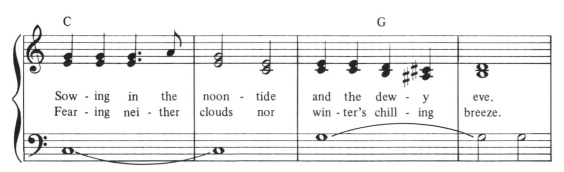

Sow - ing in the noon - tide and the dew - y eve.
Fear - ing nei - ther clouds nor win - ter's chill - ing breeze.

(Please turn the page.)

BRINGING IN THE SHEAVES (*Continued*)

Detail of *The Harvesters*.

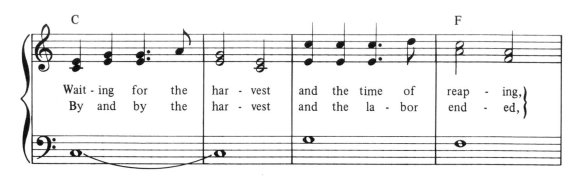

Wait - ing for the har - vest and the time of reap - ing,)
By and by the har - vest and the la - bor end - ed,}

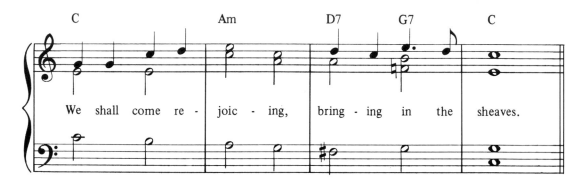

We shall come re - joic - ing, bring - ing in the sheaves.

Chorus

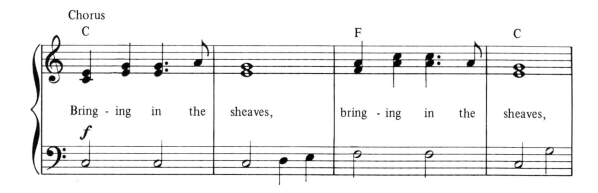

Bring - ing in the sheaves, bring - ing in the sheaves,

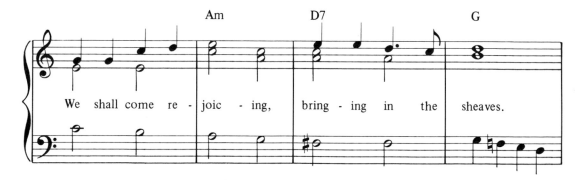

We shall come re - joic - ing, bring - ing in the sheaves.

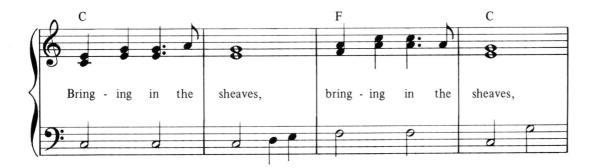

C   F   C

Bring - ing in the sheaves,   bring - ing in the sheaves,

Am   D7   G7   C   *D.C.*

We shall come re - joic - ing, bring - ing in the sheaves.

Nearly three thousand years before Bruegel's Flemish peasants lived, the ancient Egyptians harvested wheat in much the same way. This detail of a copy of a wall painting from the tomb of Sennedjem, an honored craftsman in the royal workshops, shows Sennedjem and his wife in paradise, working in the fields of the god Osiris. The Egyptians believed that afterlife for the virtuous would be a continuation of life on earth. But this is a symbolic scene. In reality, farmhands would be doing the harvesting, not this elegantly dressed couple.

Harvesting in the Fields of the Afterlife. Detail of a facsimile wall painting from the Tomb of Sennedjem (no. 1). Egyptian (Thebes), Dynasty 18, ca. 1320–1200 B.C. Tempera on paper, 1922, by C. K. Wilkinson.

CLEMENTINE

In Winslow Homer's "Camp Fire," painted in 1880, the tackle basket and net tell us that the men are on a fishing trip. They may well have known the sad story of Clementine, for the song was very popular during the Civil War. By then the Gold Rush and the forty-niners had become part of American folklore. Although Clementine and her father come to an unhappy end, we cannot help smiling at comical touches like the heroine's "number nine" shoes.

Camp Fire. Winslow Homer, American, 1836–1910. Oil on canvas, 1880.

1. In a cav - ern, in a can - yon, Ex - ca-
vat - ing for a mine, Lived a min - er, for - ty-

2. Light she was and like a fair - y, And her
shoes were num - ber nine; Her - ring box - es with - out

*Guitar: Capo 3rd fret

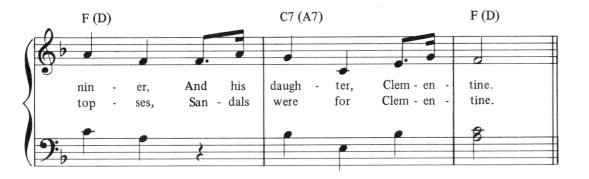

nin - er, And his daugh - ter, Clem - en - tine.
top - ses, San - dals were for Clem - en - tine.

Chorus

F (D)

Oh my dar - ling, Oh my dar - ling, Oh my

mf

C7 (A7)

dar - ling, Clem - en - tine, You are lost and gone for-

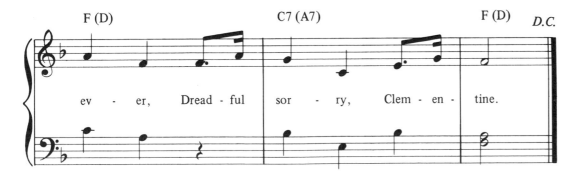

F (D)   C7 (A7)   F (D) *D.C.*

ev - er, Dread - ful sor - ry, Clem - en - tine.

Additional verses:

3.
Drove she ducklings to the water,
Ev'ry morning just at nine;
Hit her foot against a splinter,
Fell into the foaming brine.
(Chorus)

4.
Ruby lips above the water,
Blowing bubbles soft and fine;
But alas, he was no swimmer,
So he lost his Clementine.
(Chorus)

5.
Then the miner, forty-niner,
Soon began to peak and pine;
Thought he oughter join
          his daughter,
Now he's with his Clementine.
(Chorus)

The Mountain Man. Frederic Remington, American, 1861–1909. Bronze, 1903.

DID YOU EVER SEE A LASSIE?

When photography became popular in the nineteenth century, some people thought that this would mean the end of painting, but the best artists found that they could learn from the camera. For centuries, galloping horses had usually been pictured with all four legs stretched out in front and behind like the legs on a rocking horse. In 1878, Eadweard Muybridge successfully photographed a horse in motion in a series of stop-action still shots that showed how horses really move. Nine years later, he published a book that included photographs of men and women in action, too.

Moderately

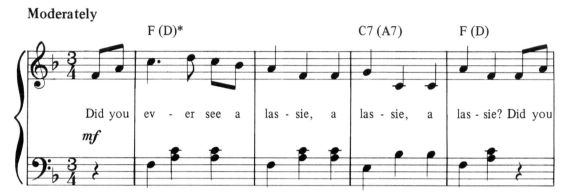

Did you ev - er see a las - sie, a las - sie, a las - sie? Did you

mf

F (D)*   C7 (A7)   F (D)

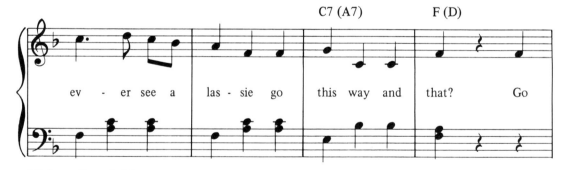

ev - er see a las - sie go this way and that? Go

C7 (A7)   F (D)

*Guitar: Capo 3rd fret

28

C7 (A7)　　F (D)　　C7 (A7)　　F (D)

this way and | that way and | this way and | that way, Did you

C7 (A7)　　F (D)

ev - er see a | las - sie go | this way and | that?

Included in the book were photographs recording the successive movements of a dance performed by a student at the University of Pennsylvania. If you look at the photos very quickly, one after the other, the woman seems to be actually moving, and Muybridge's experiments led directly to the invention of motion pictures. "Did You Ever See a Lassie?" is a very old song, and the tune comes from an even older German folk ditty. Its beat is like Muybridge's camera clicking as it records the young girl in her flowing draperies going "this way and that way and this way and that way."

Dancing Girl: A Pirouette. Eadweard Muybridge, British, 1830–1904. Collotypes from *Animal Locomotion*. Philadelphia: University of Pennsylvania, 1887.

The unknown artist who painted this delightful picture of a plantation in the old South more than 160 years ago probably never had a lesson and never learned perspective, but he put everything down so vividly that we could easily find our way to the fine mansion on top of the hill. We do not know if this estate was a real or imaginary place. Some think the scene was taken from a needlework design because of its flat pattern and the way in which the two big trees and the bunches of grapes are painted, with the brushstrokes resembling embroidery stitches. The slave quarters and other buildings are shown from the front and side at the same time, and the pool in the lower left corner makes a frame for the willow tree, so that we can see it more clearly. The beautiful ship sailing along the shore balances the shape of the house at the top of the painting.

DIXIE

With spirit ($\half$ = 1 beat)

I wish I was in the land of cot - ton,
Dix - ie Land where I was born in

Old times there are not for - got - ten. Look a - way! Look a -
Ear - ly on one frost - y morn - in'. Look a - way! Look a -

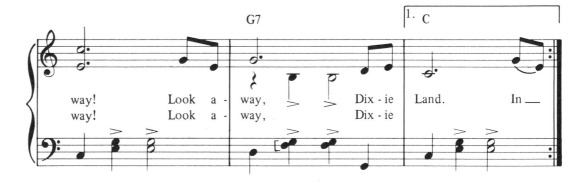

way! Look a - way, Dix - ie Land. In
way! Look a - way, Dix - ie

Chorus

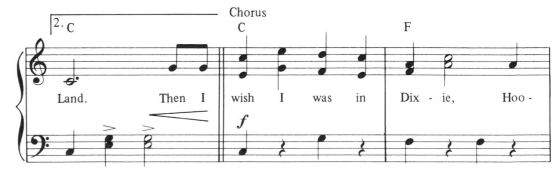

Land. Then I wish I was in Dix - ie, Hoo -

DIXIE *(Continued)*

Detail of *The Plantation*.

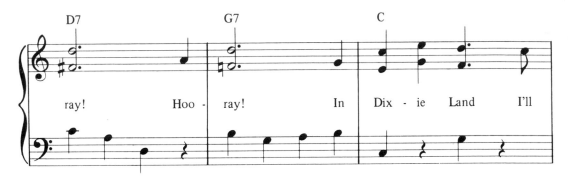

ray! Hoo - ray! In Dix - ie Land I'll

take my stand To live and die in Dix - ie. A-

way, a - way, a - way down south in Dix - ie! A-

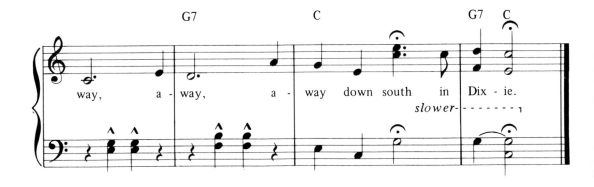

way, a - way, a - way down south in Dix - ie.

slower- - - - - - -

DOWN BY THE RIVERSIDE

The spiritual "Down by the Riverside" expresses a longing for peace and rest after the struggles of life. There is a similar mood in this haunting painting by Martin Johnson Heade, with its strange, eerie light. The dark, threatening sky warns of storms ahead, yet the solitary man with his dog finds comfort in the hushed stillness by the water's edge, and the single white sail is like a message of hope. Like the singer of the song, we all long for the day when people will "study war no more."

The Coming Storm (detail). Martin Johnson Heade, American, 1819–1904. Oil on canvas, 1859.

Moderately, with a strong beat

1. Gon - na   lay   down   my   sword   and   shield,
2. Gon - na   meet   my   Lord   Je - sus,
3. Gon - na   lay   down   my   bur - den,

Down   by   the

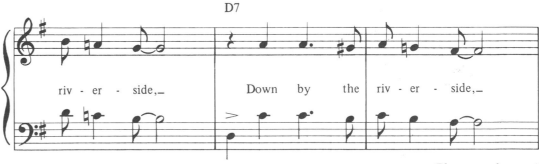

riv - er - side,   Down   by   the   riv - er - side,

(Please turn the page.)

33

DOWN BY THE RIVERSIDE *(Continued)*

Perhaps the most moving folk songs ever to come from America are spirituals like "Down by the Riverside," sung by blacks in the South in the days of slavery, sometimes accompanying ship loading or work on the plantation. The deep emotion and strong beat of the spirituals helped to make life a little more bearable in hard times. The words, usually based on stories or phrases from the Bible, evoked feelings and memories all could share, and the rhythms of the chorus were often stressed by clapping hands.

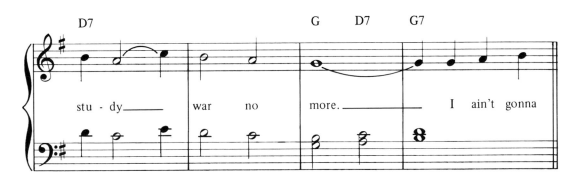

Detail of *The Coming Storm*.

34

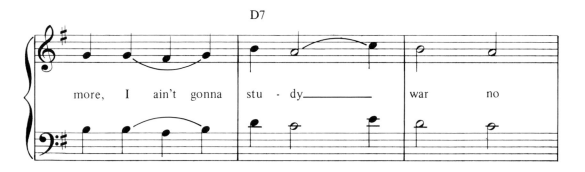

more, I ain't gonna stu - dy_____ war no

more._____ I ain't gonna stu - dy war no

Since Biblical times, the dove and the olive branch have been symbols of peace. In this detail from a Baltimore album quilt, a floral wreath surrounds a dove with an olive branch in its beak. The flowers, like the others in the quilt, are shaped from carefully chosen fabrics.

more, I ain't gonna stu - dy war no more, I ain't gonna

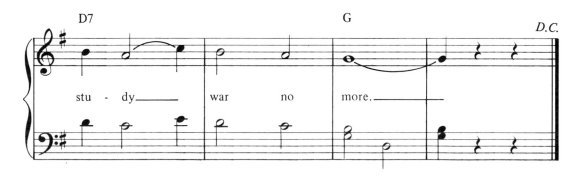

stu - dy_____ war no more._____

Dove holding an olive branch. Detail of an album quilt. American (Baltimore, Maryland). Cotton and silk appliqué, ca. 1850.

Route of the Black Diamond. Mark Baum, American, b. 1903. Oil on canvas, ca. 1940.

People were so thrilled by the invention of the steam locomotive early in the last century that they soon began to make up songs and stories about railroads and railroad workers. The second steam locomotive invented by the British engineer George Stephenson, the pioneer of railroads, was called "Puffing Billy." It was used to pull heavy loads of coal from the mines to Newcastle, and its name may have been the origin of the "puffer bellies" mentioned in the song.

For the painting above, the American artist Mark Baum set up his easel across the tracks in Ithaca, New York. The railroad line he painted was called "Route of the Black Diamond," for its main cargo was coal from the Pennsylvania mines. The picture has a feeling of "early in the morning." Although we see no trains or people, the painting delights us with its charming simplicity and with its appeal to our imagination. Even the emptiness of the station and the tracks is exciting, for at any moment we might hear the sounds of the oncoming train as it makes its way through the distant hills.

DOWN BY THE STATION

The possibilities of steam locomotion were amusingly caricatured in a British print of the 1830s by Robert Seymour, who used the name "Shortshanks." The teapot locomotive ridden by the two ladies is *truly* a "puffer belly."

Moderately

F (D)* Down by the sta - tion ear - ly in the morn - ing,

mf

See the lit - tle puf - fer bel - lies all in a row.

G7 (E7)   C7 (A7)

F (D) See the en - gine driv - er pull the lit - tle throt - tle;

C7 (A7)   F (D)

N.C. Puff, puff, Toot! Toot! Off we go.

B♭ (G)   C7 (A7)   F (D)

Locomotion (detail). Robert Seymour, British, 1798–1836. Hand-colored etching, ca. 1830.

*Guitar: Capo 3rd fret

EENSY WEENSY SPIDER

Some people are afraid of spiders, but they should not be, for most spiders are not dangerous to people and use their delicate-looking but surprisingly strong webs to catch many harmful insects. Spiders are fascinating to watch and more persevering than many human beings. The tiny spider in the song may be washed down the waterspout by the pouring rain, but as soon as the sun comes out, up he climbs again. In this painting on silk by the Japanese artist Taki Katei from an album of flower and bird studies, the spider is beginning to spin its wonderful web, stretching the thread between the branches of a fruit tree and working with the skill and persistence of an engineer.

Like a slow march

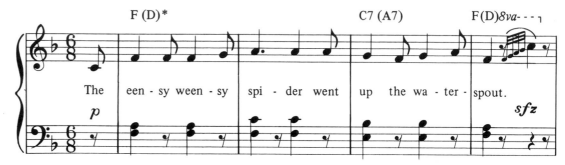

The een-sy ween-sy spi-der went up the wa-ter-spout.

Down came the rain___ and washed the spi-der out.

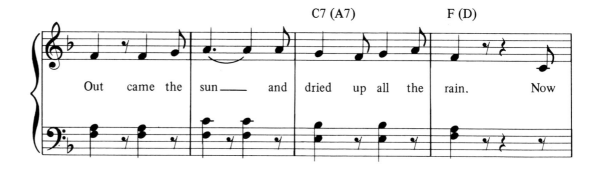

Out came the sun___ and dried up all the rain. Now

een-sy ween-sy spi-der went up the spout a-gain.

Spider (detail). From the album *Flowers and Birds.* Taki Katei, Japanese, 1832–1901. Ink and colors on silk.

*Guitar: Capo 3rd fret

THE FARMER IN THE DELL

Like a march

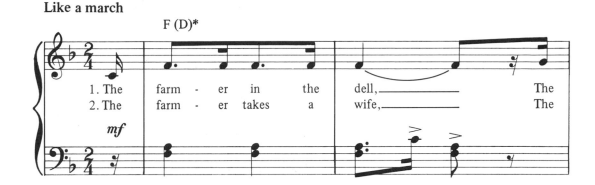

When this song was first sung, no one ever thought of painting a landscape from the air. The modern artist Yvonne Jacquette has painted several aerial views of cities and the countryside. From the window of a single-engine plane flying over Little River Farm in Belfast in southern Maine, she made three or four pastel studies, then used them as she painted in oil this bird's-eye view of the farm and its surroundings. Unlike a map, which is only a diagram, the artist's unusual point of view creates exciting patterns on the ground below while capturing the peaceful country atmosphere.

1. The farm-er in the dell,_____ The
2. The farm-er takes a wife,_____ The

farm-er in the dell,_____ Heigh - ho, the
farm-er takes a wife,_____ Heigh - ho, the

der - ry - o, The farm-er in the dell._____
der - ry - o, The farm-er takes a wife._____

*Guitar: Capo 3rd fret

Additional verses:

3.
The wife takes a child, *etc.*

4.
The child takes a nurse, *etc.*

5.
The nurse takes a dog, *etc.*

6.
The dog takes a cat, *etc.*

7.
The cat takes a rat, *etc.*

8.
The rat takes the cheese, *etc.*

9.
The cheese stands alone, *etc.*

Little River Farm (detail). Yvonne Jacquette, American, b. 1934. Oil on canvas, 1979.

THE FOX

Foxes, both the red and the gray kind, are very pretty animals, with their bright eyes, pointed snouts and ears, long bushy tails, and quick darting movements. But farmers and gardeners do not like them, for they can do a lot of damage. They are clever at stalking their prey, lying in wait until they are ready to pounce. The designer of this tapestry made the fox very hard to find among all the greenery and flowers. If you look closely, you can see that he has his eye on the golden pheasant, who would certainly make a tasty meal! The tapestry was designed by a partner of William Morris, who founded a company in England more than one hundred years ago to make beautiful furnishings as he believed people had done in the Middle Ages.

In this old folk song, the fox is up to no good. The story ends very badly for the poor gray goose and for old John and his wife, but we cannot help being amused at the thought of the mischievous fox sitting down with his wife and their ten little ones in their "cozy den" to enjoy a delicious dinner.

Greenery (detail). English. Designed in 1892 by John Henry Dearle (1860–1932). Woven in 1915 at Merton Abbey by John Martin of Morris and Company. Wool and silk.

Brightly

1. The fox went out on a chill-y night, He
2. He ran till he came to a great big bin, The

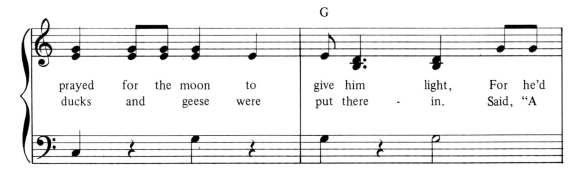

prayed for the moon to give him light, For he'd
ducks and geese were put there - in. Said, "A

man - y a mile to go that night Be - fore he reached the
cou - ple of you will grease my chin Be - fore I leave this

42

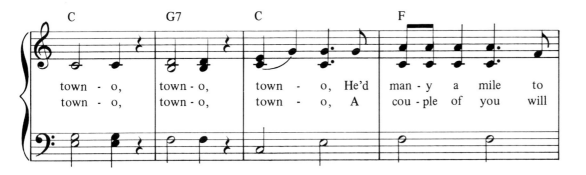

town - o, | town - o, | town - o, He'd | man - y a mile to
town - o, | town - o, | town - o, A | cou - ple of you will

go that night be - fore he reached the town - o.
grease my chin be - fore I leave this town - o."

Fox Jumping (detail). Attributed to Kawanabe Kyōsai, Japanese, 1831–1889. Ink on paper.

The Japanese artist who painted this hanging scroll chose to portray a dramatic moment, with the fox jumping in midair, possibly about to close in on its prey. With their sharp hearing and keen sense of smell, foxes can easily discover unprotected animals like the goose in the song.

Additional verses:

3.
He grabbed the gray goose by the neck,
Slung the little one down over his back,
He didn't mind at all their quack, quack, quack,
And their legs all dangling down-o,
    down-o, down-o,
He didn't mind at all their quack, quack, quack,
And their legs all dangling down-o.

4.
Old mother pitter-patter jumped out of bed,
Out of the window she cocked her head,
Crying, "John, John, the gray goose is gone
And the fox is on the town-o,
    town-o, town-o,"
Crying, "John, John, the gray goose is gone
And the fox is on the town-o."

5.
John he went to the top o' the hill,
Blew on his horn both loud and shrill,
The fox, he said, "I better flee with my kill,
He'll soon be on my trail-o, trail-o, trail-o,"
The fox, he said, "I better flee with my kill,
He'll soon be on my trail-o."

6.
He ran till he came to his cozy den,
There were the little ones, eight, nine, ten.
They said, "Daddy, you better go right back again
'Cause it must be a mighty fine town-o,
    town-o, town-o,"
They said, "Daddy, you better go right back again
'Cause it must be a mighty fine town-o."

7.
Then the fox and his wife without any strife,
They cut up the goose with a fork and knife.
They never had such a supper in their life,
And the little ones chewed on the bones-o,
    bones-o, bones-o,
They never had such a supper in their life,
And the little ones chewed on the bones-o.

A FROG WENT A-COURTIN'

Frogs are delightful to watch, whether on land or in the water. A gentleman frog looks so dashing as he leaps from one lily pad to another that it is easy to imagine him dressed up in fine clothes "with a sword and pistol by his side" going a-courting not a lady frog, but Miss Mousie! According to this version of the song, it was a very straightforward courtship, with no words wasted on either side, and we are sure the happy pair enjoyed their honeymoon in France. Other, longer versions describe the wedding festivities— in some, even what the guests had for supper.

The Chinese artist who painted this frog on a lotus leaf did so with great sensitivity, for to Chinese and Japanese artists, a bird on a twig or a beetle on a blade of grass was just as interesting a subject as something grand like a mountain. The frog crouching on his leaf among the rushes looks as if he could leap off at any moment.

Frog on a lotus leaf (detail). From the album *Landscapes, Flowers, and Birds.* Hsiang Sheng-mo, Chinese, 1597–1658. Ink and colors on paper, 1639.

Moderately (♩ = 1 beat)

F (D)*   B♭ (G)   C7 (A7)

1. A frog went a-court-in', he did ride. (Hum__
2. He rode up__ to Miss Mous-ie's den. (Hum__

mf   *lightly*

*Guitar: Capo 3rd fret

F(D)

(Hum___) A frog went a-court-in',
(Hum___) He rode up___ to Miss

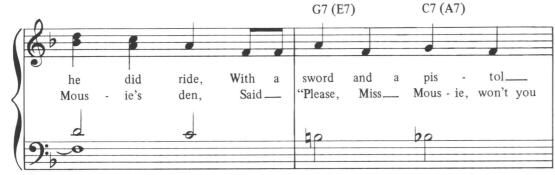

G7 (E7)   **C7 (A7)**

he did ride, With a sword and a pis - tol___
Mous - ie's den, Said___ "Please, Miss___ Mous - ie, won't you

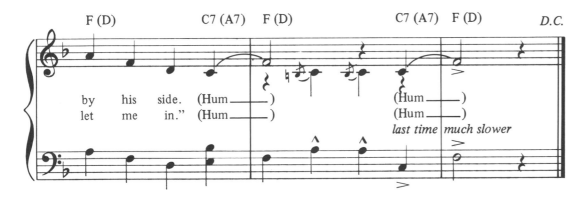

F (D)   **C7 (A7) F (D)**   **C7 (A7) F (D)**   *D.C.*

by his side. (Hum___)   (Hum___)
let me in." (Hum___)   (Hum___)

last time | much slower

Frog automaton. Swiss, ca. 1820. Gold and enamel with rubies and pearls.

T his little frog, studded with rubies and pearls, is an automaton. When its clockwork mechanism is activated, the frog not only moves its legs and goes forward on tiny wheels, but it also croaks!

Additional verses:

3.
"Yes, Sir Frog, I sit and spin. (hum)
Yes, Sir Frog, I sit and spin,
Please, Mr. Froggie, won't you come in?"
   (hum)

4.
The froggie said, "My dear, I've come to see,"
   (hum)
The froggie said, "My dear, I've come to see
If you, Miss Mousie, will marry me." (hum)

5.
"Oh, yes, Sir Frog, I'll marry you. (hum)
Oh, yes, Sir Frog, I'll marry you,
And we'll have children two by two." (hum)

6.
The frog and mouse they went to France.
   (hum)
The frog and mouse they went to France,
And that's the end of my romance. (hum)

46

GO IN AND OUT THE WINDOW

Brightly, with spirit

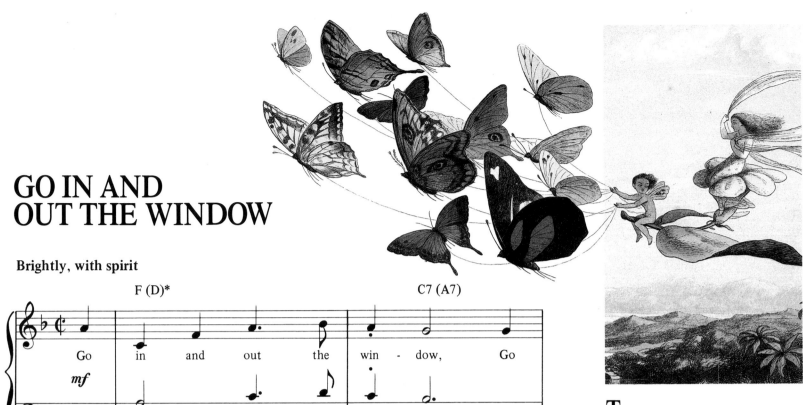

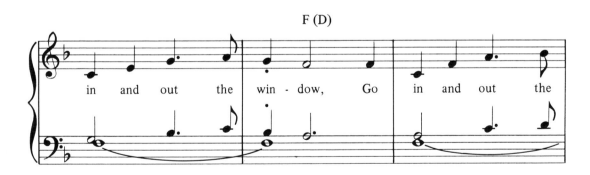

Go in and out the win-dow, Go

in and out the win-dow, Go in and out the

win-dow As we have done be-fore.

*Guitar: Capo 3rd fret

This little ditty is as cheerful as the sunny room in the illustration by Franz M. Melchers. The picture is from a book describing in verses and pictures the months of the year and its changing seasons. Other pictures in the book show the gentle countryside of Holland and its windmills and canals.

The song is an old favorite, and children enjoy inventing additional verses, such as "Go round and round the village," "Stand and face your partner," and "Go up and down the staircase."

The Fairy Queen (detail). Richard Doyle, British, 1824–1883. Chromolithograph from *In Fairyland, A Series of Pictures from the Elf-World*. London: Longmans, Green, Reader and Dyer, 1870.

Hand-tinted lithograph from *L'An*. Franz M. Melchers, Belgian, 1868–1944. Brussels: E. Lyon-Claesen, 1897.

GREEN GROW THE RUSHES-O

This song comes from Ireland, where people love folk music and ballads and where "the wearing of the green" is part of the national tradition. The verses get longer as they go from one to twelve, and some of the symbols, such as the four gospels and the ten commandments, are religious.

Arques-la-Bataille (detail).
John H. Twachtman, American, 1853–1902.
Oil on canvas, 1885.

The twelve verses of this song are sung in cumulative fashion:
   First verse = I'll sing you one-o, Green grow the rushes-o, What is your one-o?
         followed by the material labeled ①.
   Second verse = I'll sing you two-o, Green grow the rushes-o, What is your two-o?
         followed by the material labeled ②, *then* ① *is repeated.*
   Third verse continues in similar fashion: ③ ② ①.
   Other verses continue until the twelfth verse, which includes all the material in the song.

Moderately and rather freely throughout

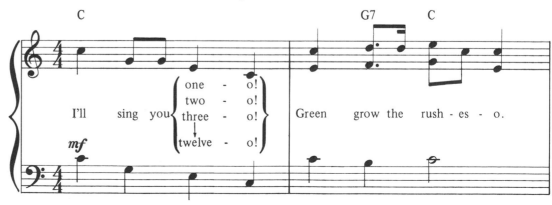

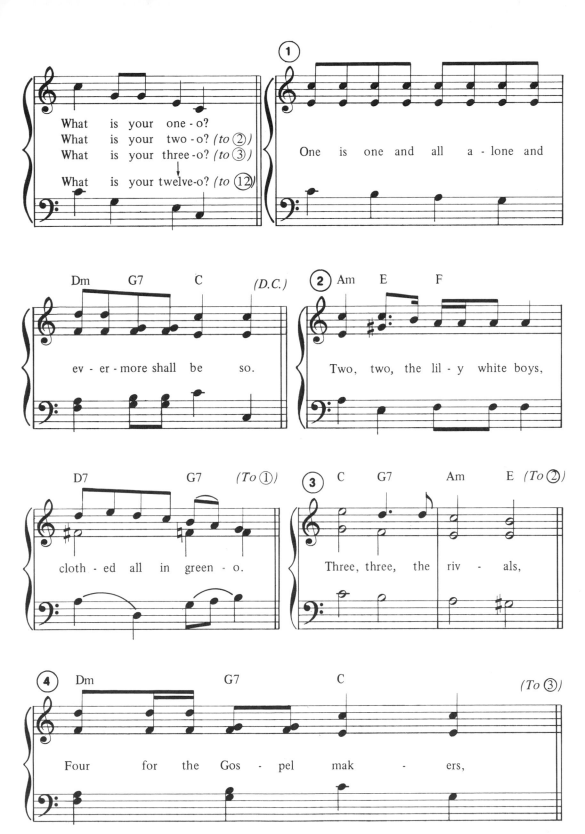

The soft bluish greens of the French landscape around Dieppe on the Normandy coast have been captured here by the American Impressionist artist John H. Twachtman. He chose to paint the riverbank on a gray day, and the picture has a cool, restful mood and atmosphere, with the silvery tones of the water adding to the effect. For an artist, painting a landscape under gray skies can be just as exciting as painting the same scene in bright sunlight.

For Twachtman, this was an important painting. He wrote to his friend, the American artist J. Alden Weir, that he had spent a month painting a large canvas for the French Salon, an exhibition held each year in Paris. The painting's large size (it is five feet high and more than six-and-a-half feet long) would have helped it stand out among the other paintings in the show. Although the Salon rejected Twachtman's work, it is today considered to be his masterpiece.

(Please turn the page.)

GREEN GROW THE RUSHES-O *(Continued)*

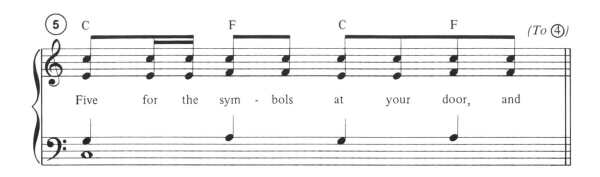

5 C   F   C   F   *(To ④)*

Five   for   the   sym - bols   at   your   door,   and

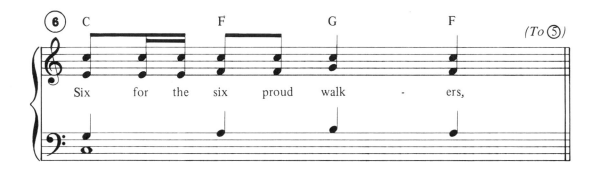

6 C   F   G   F   *(To ⑤)*

Six   for   the   six   proud   walk -   ers,

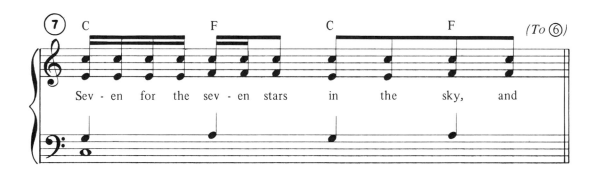

7 C   F   C   F   *(To ⑥)*

Sev - en   for   the   sev - en stars   in   the   sky,   and

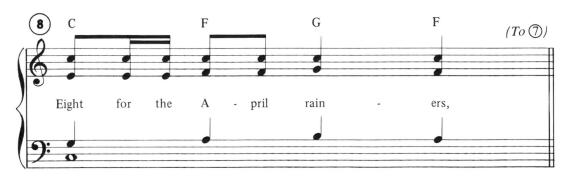

8 C   F   G   F   *(To ⑦)*

Eight   for   the   A - pril   rain -   ers,

Autumn Grasses. Detail from a six-panel screen. Japanese, mid-17th century. Colors and gold leaf on paper.

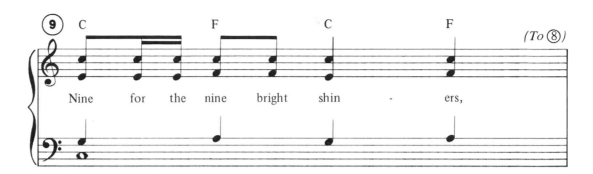

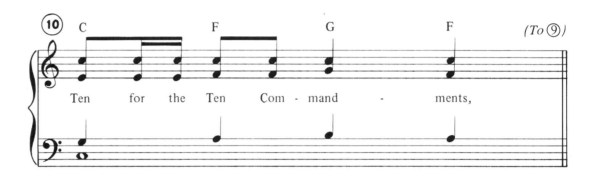

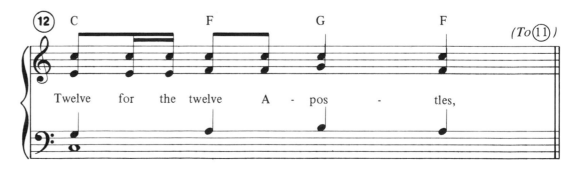

Chantons sur lebette
auec ta mulette
quelque note double

Tuant est de georgette
elle a labour nette
mes ie fais le touble

GREENSLEEVES

Moderately flowing

Long, long ago, people used to make their own music. Not only professional musicians, but nearly everyone could sing and play an instrument, from great lords and ladies to simple peasants like the shepherd and shepherdess in this tapestry. As they sit under a fruit tree in a meadow full of flowers, the shepherd plays a small bagpipe called a musette, while the shepherdess accompanies him with a song. It is a peaceful scene, with the shepherd's dog sleeping beside him and birds flying overhead. The shepherdess seems more interested in her music than in the shepherd. In the writing above him, he grumbles that while she has a lovely voice, it is he, puffing away at his bagpipe, who is doing all the work.

"Greensleeves" was a favorite song in the days of England's great Queen Elizabeth I, and Shakespeare mentions it in one of his plays. It may even date from the time of Elizabeth's father, King Henry VIII, who himself composed songs. It is a melancholy tune and the words are sad, for the singer complains that although he and his lady were once friends and he gave her beautiful presents, she no longer cares for him. Even so, he still loves her and hopes she will come back to him.

1. A- las, my love, you do me wrong to
2. I have been read-y at your hand to

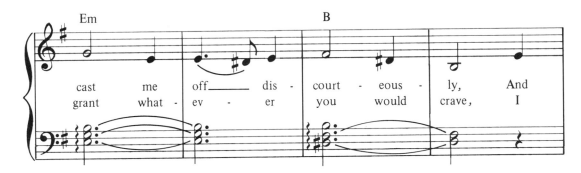

cast me off dis- court- eous- ly, And
grant what- ev- er you would crave, I

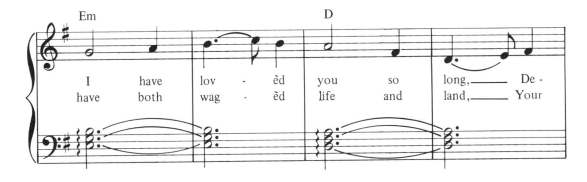

I have lov- èd you so long, De-
have both wag- èd life and land, Your

light- ing in your com- pa- ny.
love and good will for to have.

Millefleurs tapestry (detail).
Franco-Flemish, late 15th century.
Wool and silk.

(Please turn the page.)

GREENSLEEVES *(Continued)*

Chorus

G Green - sleeves was all my joy, **D**

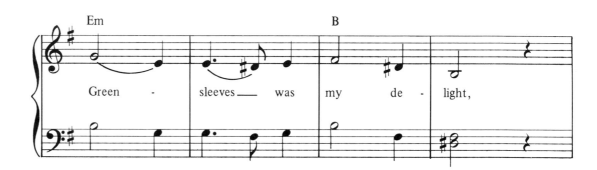

Em Green - sleeves was my de - light, **B**

G Green - sleeves, my heart of gold, **D** And

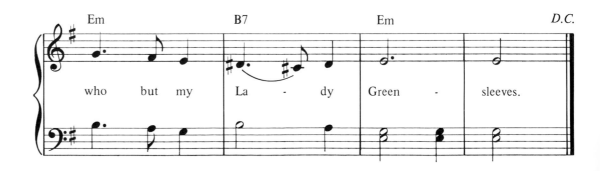

Em who but my **B7** La - dy **Em** Green - sleeves. *D.C.*

This drawing of a plump bagpipe player seated on a rough three-legged stool has been attributed to Pieter Brueghel the Younger, elder son of the great Pieter Bruegel who painted "The Harvesters." During the kermis, an annual fete and fair celebrated by the Flemish peasantry, villagers danced to the tunes of traveling bag-pipers, drank home-brewed beer, and bought housewares and trinkets from booths set up by itinerant merchants.

Seated Man Playing Bagpipes (detail). Attributed to Pieter Brueghel the Younger, Flemish, 1564–1638. Pen and brown ink.

Tall clock. Movement by Benjamin Willard, 1743–1803, and Simon Willard, 1754–1849. American (Roxbury, Massachusetts). Mahogany and brass, 1772.

The men who built movements, dials, and pendulums for grandfather clocks often signed their work, but the cabinetmakers who built the cases that enclose them are today largely unknown. The inscriptions on the dial and movement of this handsome example tell us that they were made in 1772 for James Mears by Benjamin and Simon Willard. They even state that it was Benjamin's hundred-and-thirty-first clock, made in Simon's seventeenth year.

Jerboa mouse. Egyptian, Dynasty 12, ca. 1991–1786 B.C. White and brown faience.

HICKORY, DICKORY, DOCK

Moderately (♩. = 1 beat)

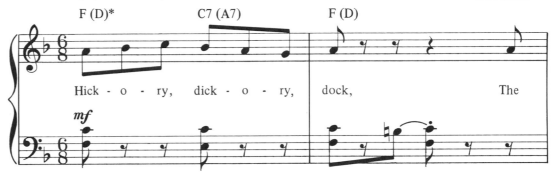

Hick - o - ry, dick - o - ry, dock, The

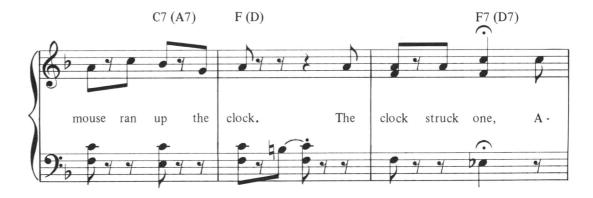

mouse ran up the clock. The clock struck one, A-

way he run! Hick - o - ry, dick - o - ry, dock.

*Guitar: Capo 3rd fret

*The Rocky Mountains,
Lander's Peak* (detail).
Albert Bierstadt,
American, 1830–1902.
Oil on canvas, 1863.

Americans have always been drawn to wide open spaces, and from pioneer days to the present the West has had a special appeal. Albert Bierstadt was one of several artists who painted Western scenery, and his canvases of the Rockies and the Yosemite Valley were immensely popular. On the first of his westward journeys, he accompanied Colonel F. W. Lander's expedition to the Rocky Mountains in Wyoming, where he collected material for this large, panoramic landscape, painted in his studio after his return to New York. As he worked, Bierstadt used sketches and studies made on the spot, as well as photo-graphs, combining exact detail with a feeling of the grand sweep of the mountain range. Bierstadt actually saw and sketched the Shoshone Indians that appear in the painting. He wrote that they "are still as they were hundreds of years ago, and now is the time to paint them," for he feared that they and their culture were rapidly dying out.

Frontier life was often hard and rough, but "Home on the Range" makes it seem quite romantic. Buffalo, deer, and other animals roam and graze over the land under a cloudless sky, while everyone is friendly and helpful.

HOME ON THE RANGE

Moderately

Oh, give me a home where the buf - fa - lo roam, Where the

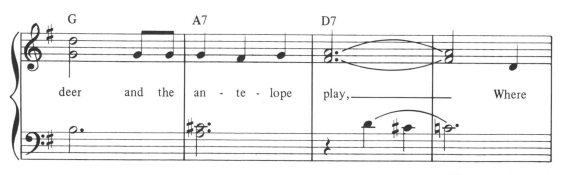

deer and the an - te - lope play, _____ Where

(Please turn the page.)

HOME ON THE RANGE *(Continued)*

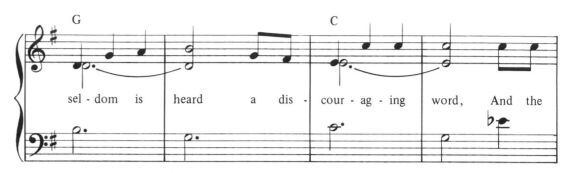

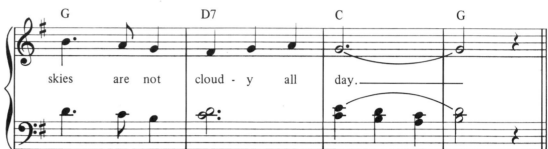

sel - dom is heard a dis - cour - ag - ing word, And the

skies are not cloud - y all day.

Africa. Maurice Heaton, American, b. 1900.
Enameled glass bowl, 1949.

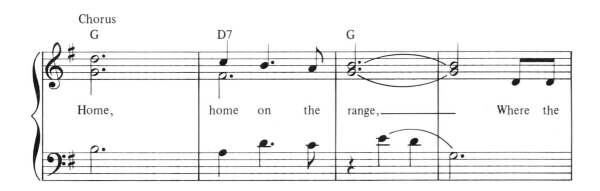

Chorus

Home, home on the range, Where the

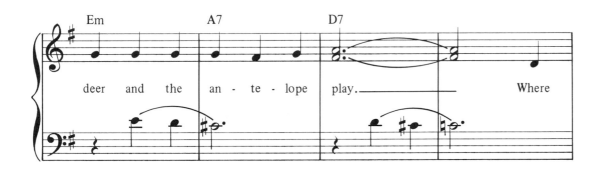

deer and the an- te- lope play. Where

sel -dom is heard a dis -cour -ag -ing word, And the

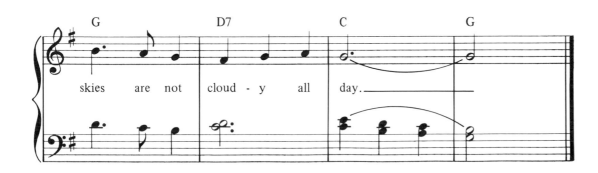

skies are not cloud -y all day.

My Bunkie (detail). Charles Schreyvogel, American, 1861–1912. Oil on canvas, ca. 1899.

Victorian Interior II (detail). Horace Pippin,
American, 1888–1946. Oil on canvas, 1945.

HOME SWEET HOME

This interior by the black artist
Horace Pippin has no people in it,
yet it seems very much alive. Pippin,
a self-taught artist, did not begin to
paint until he was forty-two, but for
years he had drawn the people and
things around him. All his life he
worked as much from imagination
and memory as from what he actually
saw.

As the song suggests, we all
remember something of the home in
which we grew up. This picture,
however, is not of any one place, but
is instead a combination of several
rooms remembered by Pippin from
his early days. The solid furniture
and the heavy frames are typically
Victorian, and so are the delicate lace
antimacassars placed on the backs of
the armchairs to prevent them from
getting soiled by people's hair.

Slowly

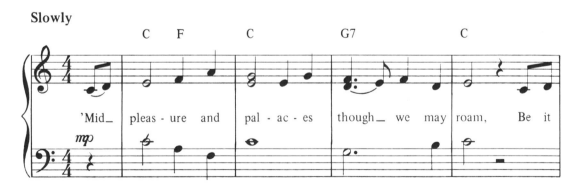

'Mid_ pleas - ure and pal - ac - es though_ we may roam, Be it

ev - er so hum - ble, there's no____ place like home. A

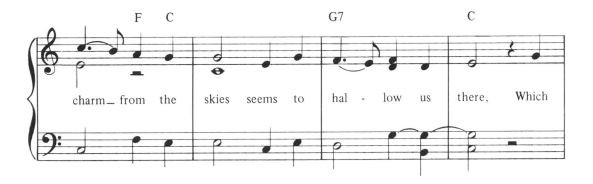

charm_ from the skies seems to hal - low us there, Which

seek_ through the world, is ne'er met_ with else - where.

Chorus

Home! Home!_ Sweet, sweet home! Be it

ev - er so hum - ble, there's no_ place like home._

Although the Victorian interiors of one-hundred years ago were often very fussy and cluttered, Pippin has painted this room in a bold and simple manner. Each piece of furniture, dark against the light wall, stands out very clearly. Everything faces front—even the flowers in the vase—and we can tell that the artist enjoyed painting the scene. He balances one side of the picture against the other, making the composition restful but not boring. Pippin had seen pictures by the great French artist Henri Matisse, who loved pattern, and perhaps that is why Pippin painted the design in the rug in such a delightful way.

Cross-stitch sampler. American, 19th century. Wool on cotton ground.

HUSH, LITTLE BABY

Babies love being sung to, even if they cannot understand the words, and repetition delights them, just as they enjoy hearing the same story over and over again when they are a little older. This gentle, playful lullaby tells of one delightful present after another. Although none of them may quite work out, and even the horse and cart may fall down, the baby will still be the sweetest in town—its parents' love is the greatest and most lasting gift of all.

Gently

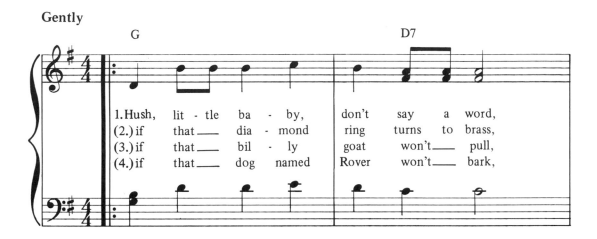

1. Hush, lit - tle ba - by, don't say a word,
(2.) if that___ dia - mond ring turns to brass,
(3.) if that___ bil - ly goat won't___ pull,
(4.) if that___ dog named Rover won't___ bark,

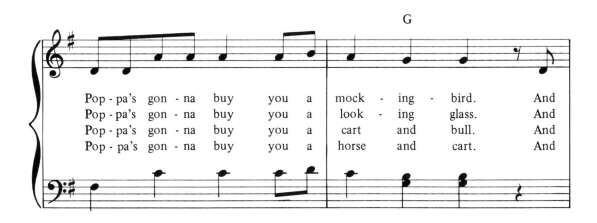

Pop - pa's gon - na buy you a mock - ing - bird. And
Pop - pa's gon - na buy you a look - ing glass. And
Pop - pa's gon - na buy you a cart and bull. And
Pop - pa's gon - na buy you a horse and cart. And

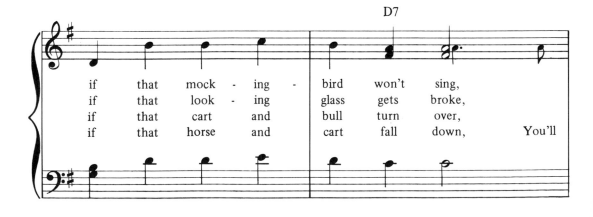

if that mock - ing - bird won't sing,
if that look - ing glass gets broke,
if that cart and bull turn over,
if that horse and cart fall down, You'll

Looking glass. American (New York), ca. 1795. Mahogany and gilt gesso.

"Just Moved" by Henry Mosler is the kind of sentimental, storytelling picture that was much more popular years ago than it is today. The objects scattered around the room, the rolled mattress, the washtub, and other details give us a fascinating glimpse of the daily life of a modest American family about to settle in their new home more than one hundred years ago. The father seated on the table slicing a loaf of bread and the mother in her rocking chair look at their baby with the same smiling, tender affection that we hear in the words and music of the lullaby.

For additional verses G *D.C.*

Pop - pa's gon - na buy you a dia - mond ring. 2. And
Pop - pa's gon - na buy you a bil - ly goat. 3. And
Pop - pa's gon - na buy you a dog named Rover. 4. And

Mockingbird. Dorothy Doughty, English, 1893–1963. Bone china. Manufactured at the Worcester Porcelain Factory, England.

Last time D7 G

still be the sweet - est lit - tle ba - by in town.

Just Moved (detail). Henry Mosler, American, 1841–1920. Oil on canvas, 1870.

I HAD A LITTLE NUT TREE

Not too fast, with a lilt

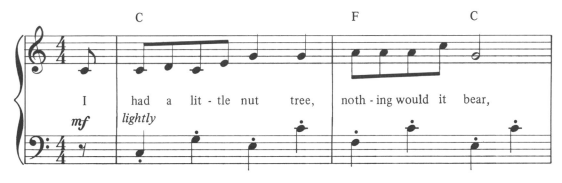

I had a lit-tle nut tree, noth-ing would it bear,

mf *lightly*

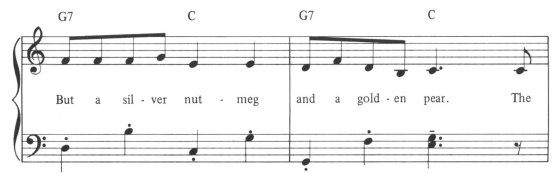

But a sil-ver nut - meg and a gold-en pear. The

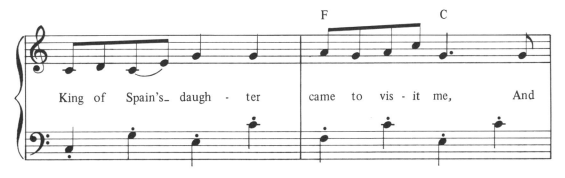

King of Spain's_ daugh - ter came to vis - it me, And

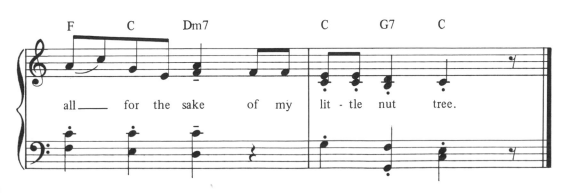

all ___ for the sake of my lit - tle nut tree.

Some people think that this song, with its soft, gentle melody, refers to a visit by Juana of Castile, daughter of King Ferdinand V of Spain, to the English court in 1506. But the words of the song make the event seem like a fairy tale, for only a magical tree could bear a silver nutmeg and a golden pear. Maria Teresa, the little princess in the painting, was the daughter of a later king of Spain. When the Infanta, as the Spanish king's daughter was called, was twenty-two, she was married to the King of France. Although Maria Teresa was still a child when this picture was painted, she was already dressed like a grown-up. She wears a grand black and silver costume with a wide, stiff skirt and a fine lace collar. The red bow and cap add the only touches of bright color. The Spanish court was very formal, and the Infanta could hardly run around and play in such a dress, but we are told that she loved to dance. She must surely have enjoyed her charming little dog.

Bird in a pear tree. Detail of an embroidered picture. English, third quarter 17th century. Silk and metal threads and pearls on satin.

Infanta Maria Teresa of Spain (1638–1683). Juan Bautista Martínez del Mazo, Spanish, ca. 1612–1667. Oil on canvas.

I LOVE
LITTLE PUSSY

This is one of the most popular nursery songs, both in England and in the United States. Children love kittens, puppies, and other small animals, but they sometimes play with them too roughly. They forget that they are not toys, and that they have feelings. This rhyme tells us that if we are kind and gentle to our pets they will be loving companions, and there is certainly no happier sound than a kitten purring by the fireside.

Gently

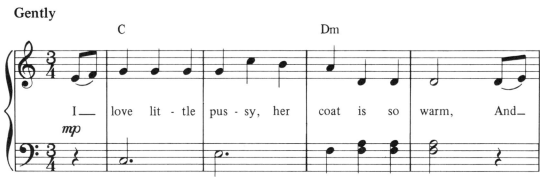

I love lit-tle pus-sy, her coat is so warm, And

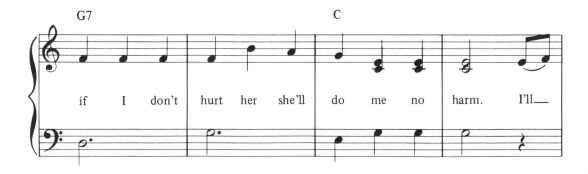

if I don't hurt her she'll do me no harm. I'll

The Chinese artist who painted this charming scene on a silk scroll must have watched many kittens at play and noted their every little movement and expression. In the scroll, five kittens are playing or relaxing in a garden, each with its own personality. A white kitten lolls on its back on a grassy tuft playing with a flowering branch. Another, part tabby, sits among flowers licking its paw. A third kitten, not shown here, is white with black and orange spots and proudly carries a bird in its mouth. A white kitten crouching behind hollyhocks gazes up at a bird in a tree, probably wondering if it is within reach! Especially endearing is a fifth kitten pictured peacefully napping.

Spring Play in a T'ang Garden. Details from a handscroll. Chinese, Ch'ing Dynasty (1644–1911). Colors on silk, ca. 18th century.

It is wonderful to see how the Japanese artist Andō Hiroshige has used the fine lines of a woodcut to create the effect of a sudden shower on a summer day. With very few colors he makes us feel the damp, chilly atmosphere under the dark rain clouds. To protect themselves, some of the people scurrying across the wooden bridge huddle under paper parasols. Another person and the man steering the raft wear broad-brimmed straw hats. While the old man in the song keeps warm and dry snoring in bed, these folks probably wish that the rain would go away.

A Sudden Shower at Ōhashi (detail). Andō Hiroshige, Japanese, 1797–1858. Woodblock print from *One Hundred Views of Edo,* 1857.

IT'S RAINING, IT'S POURING

Wistfully

It's rain - ing, it's pour - ing, The

old man is snor - ing. He went to bed and he

bumped his head, And he would-n't get up in the morn - ing.

I'VE BEEN WORKING ON THE RAILROAD

Like a slow march

I've been work-ing on the rail-road All the live-long

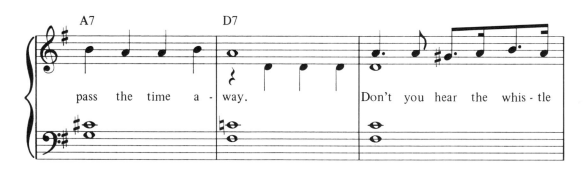

day, I've been work-ing on the rail-road Just to

pass the time a-way. Don't you hear the whis-tle

blow-ing? Rise up so ear-ly in the morn.

(Please turn the page.)

Railroads have played such an important part in the expansion of the United States, and especially in the opening of the West, that it is no wonder they have inspired so many folk songs and works of art. This popular and hearty song has the robust spirit of the early builders of the railroads. In 1913, the Norwegian-born American painter Jonas Lie traveled to Panama to observe the digging of the Panama Canal, which was to connect the Atlantic and Pacific oceans. In his painting, "The Conquerors," Lie chose a striking and unusual viewpoint from above to convey the drama and magnitude of the achievement. We see the locomotives puffing great clouds of smoke as they forge their way through Culebra Cut. The workers in the foreground climbing the hill are dwarfed by the mighty cliffs, yet the picture's title tells us that it is they who are daring to conquer nature.

At first the song makes Dinah sound like a tooting horn, but then the scene moves to the kitchen where a real, live Dinah is being entertained by her friend strumming on his banjo. What a welcome glimpse of home after a long and exhausting day's work on the railroad tracks!

The Conquerors (Culebra Cut, Panama Canal). Jonas Lie, American, 1880–1940. Oil on canvas, 1913.

71

I'VE BEEN WORKING ON THE RAILROAD *(Continued)*

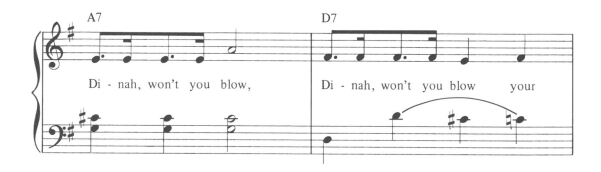

Lewis Hine, an American sociologist, took up photography in 1905 to record the plight of poor European immigrants. Some of his most powerful photographs are from the early 1920s. In the photograph seen here, he created a fine composition out of the machine and the muscular man turning a bolt. Hine admired the dignity and strong features of steel workers and other men in industry.

Powerhouse Mechanic. Lewis Hine, American, 1874–1940. Gelatin-silver print, 1925.

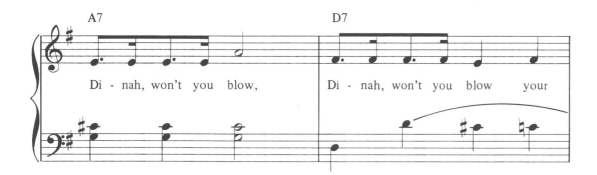

Di - nah, won't you blow,   Di - nah, won't you blow   your

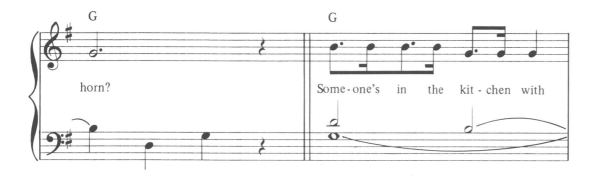

horn?   Some - one's   in   the   kit - chen   with

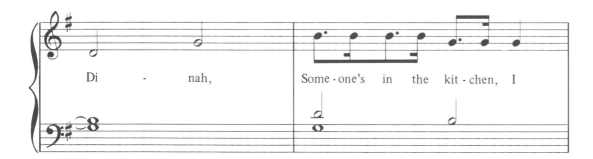

Di   -   nah,   Some - one's   in   the   kit - chen,   I

know,_____   Some - one's   in   the   kit - chen   with

Railroad Man (detail). Lewis Hine,
American, 1874–1940. Gelatin-silver print.

(Please turn the page.)

I'VE BEEN WORKING ON THE RAILROAD *(Continued)*

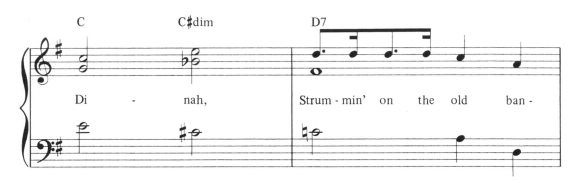

Di - nah, Strum - min' on the old ban -

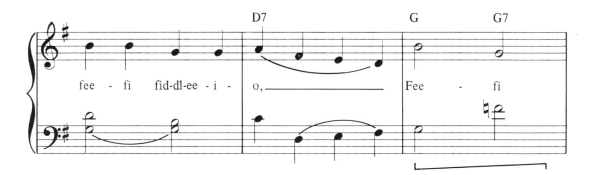

jo. (He's strum - min') Fee - fi fid-dl-ee - i - o,

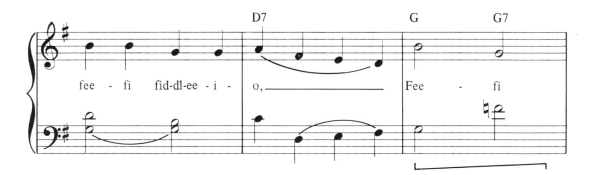

fee - fi fid-dl-ee - i - o, _____ Fee - fi

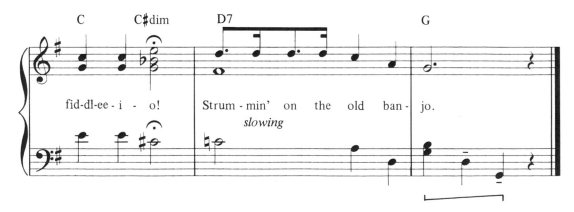

fid-dl-ee - i - o! Strum - min' on the old ban - jo.
slowing

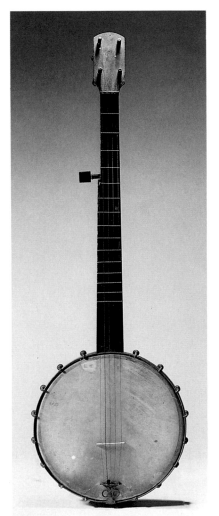

Banjo. American, ca. 1890.
Wood, parchment, and metal.

74

JACK AND JILL

In some collections of nursery rhymes published in the nineteenth century, the story of Jack and Jill and their misadventure was extended to fifteen verses, but usually only the two printed here are sung. The "vinegar and brown paper" that their mother applied to Jack's head injury seems a very rough form of first aid, but it probably worked well enough. Jill evidently did not have such a bad fall as her brother, and one version of the rhyme has a third verse in which she laughs at poor Jack with his "paper plaster" and is punished by her mother for being so unsympathetic.

Children of the Empire. Valerie Grienauer, Austrian, active in the 1920s. Stencil-colored linocut.

Moderately (♩.= 1 beat)

1. Jack and Jill went up the hill, To fetch a pail of water. Jack fell down and broke his crown, And Jill came tumbling after.

2. Up Jack got and home he ran, As fast as he could caper. There his mother bound his head, With vinegar and brown paper.

JENNIE JENKINS

Sometimes it seems more difficult to make up one's mind about something unimportant than about more serious matters. In this lighthearted old folk song, young Jennie simply cannot decide what color dress to wear, and she turns down one suggestion after another. She only knows what she does *not* want.

The pretty girl in the painting by the Viennese artist Gustav Klimt also looks hard to please and perhaps a little spoiled. However, the pale blue ribbons in her hair are very becoming, and the attractive rose pattern on her white dress picks up the colors in the carpet and on the wall. Her father was connected with a famous design workshop in Vienna, so there were many patterns from which to choose.

When songs have been around for a long time, the words often vary. In one version of "Jennie Jenkins," when Jennie, having found no color to her liking, is asked "Then what *will* you wear, oh my dear, oh my dear?" she replies cheekily, "Oh, what do I care if I just go bare?" which her family and friends no doubt thought was a very bad idea!

Mäda Primavesi. Gustav Klimt, Austrian, 1862–1918. Oil on canvas, 1912.

Brightly   F (D)*   C7 (A7)

1. Oh, will you wear blue, oh my dear, oh my dear? Oh,
2. Oh, will you wear green, oh my dear, oh my dear? Oh,

*Guitar: Capo 3rd fret

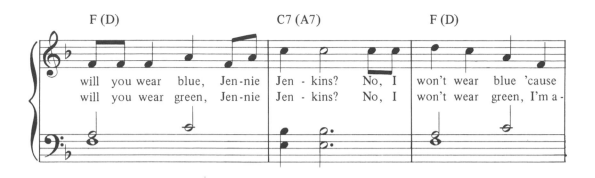

F (D)   C7 (A7)   F (D)

will you wear blue, Jen-nie Jen - kins? No, I won't wear blue 'cause
will you wear green, Jen-nie Jen - kins? No, I won't wear green, I'm a-

B♭ (G)   C7 (A7)   F (D)   Gm (Em)   F (D)

blue won't do,
shamed to be seen, } But I'll buy me a fol-ly rol-ly til-ly tol-ly

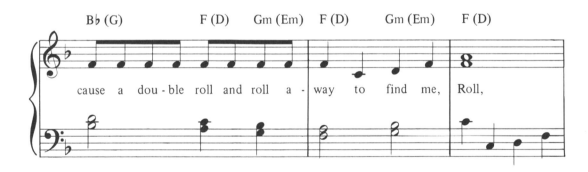

B♭ (G)   F (D)   Gm (Em)   F (D)   Gm (Em)   F (D)

cause a dou-ble roll and roll a - way to find me, Roll,

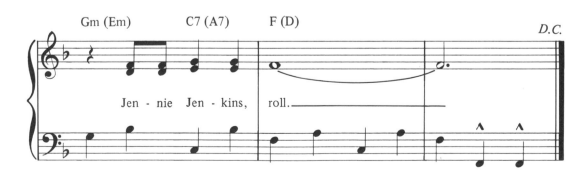

Gm (Em)   C7 (A7)   F (D)   *D.C.*

Jen - nie Jen - kins, roll.

"Belle of Newport" paper-doll costumes. Marguerite McDonald,
British. London: Raphael Tuck & Sons Company, Ltd., © 1894.

Additional verses:

3.
Oh, will you wear white. . .
It don't suit me right. . .

4.
Oh, will you wear yeller. . .
It won't get me no feller. . .

5.
Oh, will you wear red. . .
It's the color of my head. . .

LAVENDER'S BLUE

There is a "let's pretend" feeling about this nursery song. Words like "dilly dilly" make no sense, and lavender is never green, but we enjoy the way the words sound and fit in with the rhyme. The little boy singing imagines himself and his playmate growing up to be a fairy-tale king and queen.

There is the same dreamy, happy mood in the painting by the French artist Jean Baptiste Pater of seven children playing in the open air. The colors of their clothes and of the gentle landscape are as soft and delicate as those in the song. One little girl holds up a pinwheel to catch the breeze, three other children have hobbyhorses, and while some tumble to the ground as they play, no one gets hurt and a friendly dog joins in the fun.

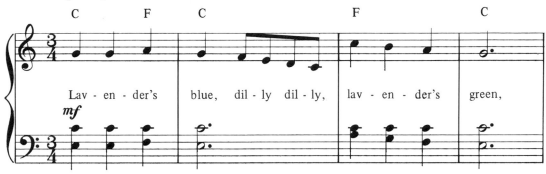

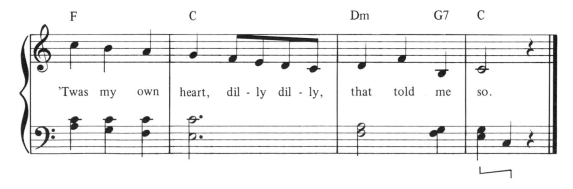

Pas de Trois. Model by Joseph Nees, German, active ca. 1754–73. Working at Ludwigsburg 1759–68. Hard-paste porcelain, ca. 1763.

The Golden Age (detail). Jean Baptiste Pater, French, 1695–1736. Oil on wood.

LAZY MARY

Getting up in the morning is never easy, and this song may have started in England as a game, with one or more children being "mother" and another child or children playing "Mary" and pretending to be fast asleep. In one version of "Lazy Mary," the mother, after trying in vain to rouse her daughter, tells her that there is a nice young man waiting for her downstairs. Then Mary quickly replies, "Yes, mother, I *will* get up!"

Perhaps the pretty shepherdess in this picture by the French court painter François Boucher will not mind being awakened when she sees the handsome young shepherd who is tickling her neck. It is unlikely, however, that she will work very hard minding her sheep, for Boucher did not paint real country people. These two are more like courtiers in fancy dress playing at being shepherd and shepherdess in a make-believe landscape where it never rains.

Briskly (♩.= 1 beat)

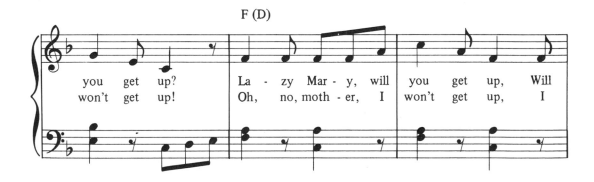

*Guitar: Capo 3rd fret

The Interrupted Sleep (detail). François Boucher, French, 1703–1770. Oil on canvas, 1750.

80

This song has many verses, and at parties children often sing them and act them out. The real London Bridge has a long history. For centuries, it was the only bridge over the River Thames. The earliest one was made of wood, but in the Middle Ages it was replaced by a stone bridge with houses and a chapel on it. There was a fortified gate at each end, where heads of people who had been executed were stuck on pikes as a warning. The bridge was often damaged by fire, and after six hundred years it *was* true that London Bridge was falling down. A new bridge was built, and this color print shows its opening in 1831, with flags flying and crowds of people watching the ceremony in boats and from the riverbanks. Those in the basket of the balloon have the best view! In recent years, even this bridge was not strong enough for modern traffic, and in 1967 work was begun on yet another one. The bridge of 1831 was pulled down in 1970 and sold to two American businessmen for almost two-and-a-half million dollars. In 1971, they built it up again, stone by stone, in Lake Havasu City, Arizona.

New London Bridge, As It Appeared August 1st, 1831. Thomas Sidney Cooper, British, 1803–1902. Hand-colored lithograph, 1831.

Moderately

F (D)*

1. Lon - don Bridge is fall - ing down,
2. Build it up with gold and sil - ver,

C7 (A7)

Fall - ing down,
Gold and sil - ver,

F (D)

fall - ing down,
gold and sil - ver,

F (D)

Lon - don Bridge is
Build it up with

fall - ing down,
gold and sil - ver,

C7 (A7)

My fair
My fair

F (D)

la - dy.
la - dy.

F (D)

Build it up with
Take the key and

i - ron bars,
lock her up,

C7 (A7)

I - ron bars,
Lock her up,

F (D)

i - ron bars,
lock her up,

Build it up with
Take the key and

i - ron bars,
lock her up,

C7 (A7)

My fair
My fair

F (D)

la - dy.
la - dy.

D.C.

LONDON BRIDGE

*Guitar: Capo 3rd fret

THE MULBERRY BUSH

Quickly (♩. = 1 beat)

Long before the days of washing machines and electricity, laundry was done by hand. In the country, clothes were washed in rivers or in wooden tubs in the garden, as this French peasant woman is doing in Camille Pissarro's painting on the right. Then the washing would be pinned on clotheslines or hung over bushes to dry, while everyone hoped there would be no rain.

Pissarro, with his fresh colors and lively dabs of paint, has captured the feeling of the outdoors, and the quiet figure of the washerwoman blends beautifully with her surroundings.

1. Here we go round the mul-ber-ry bush, The
2. This is the way we wash our clothes, We

mul-ber-ry bush, the mul-ber-ry bush, Here we go round the
wash our clothes, we wash our clothes, This is the way we

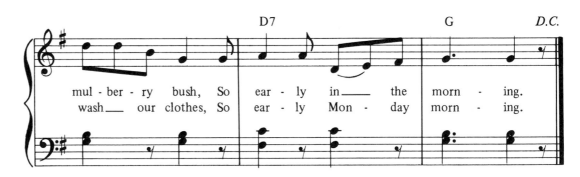

mul-ber-ry bush, So ear-ly in the morn-ing.
wash our clothes, So ear-ly Mon-day morn-ing.

A Woman Ironing (detail). Edgar Degas,
French, 1834–1917. Oil on canvas.

A Washerwoman at Eragny.
Camille Pissarro, French, 1830–1903.
Oil on canvas, 1893.

Additional verses:

3.
This is the way we iron our clothes, *etc.*
So early Tuesday morning.

4.
This is the way we scrub the floor, *etc.*
So early Wednesday morning.

5.
This is the way we mend our clothes, *etc.*
So early Thursday morning.

6.
This is the way we sweep the house, *etc.*
So early Friday morning.

7.
This is the way we bake our bread, *etc.*
So early Saturday morning.

8.
This is the way we go to church, *etc.*
So early Sunday morning.

85

MY BONNIE LIES OVER THE OCEAN

Nearly everyone has dreamed of crossing the ocean to faraway places. Often after a stay overseas a sailor or traveler becomes homesick, while those on shore look forward eagerly to their loved one's return. When this song was written—no one knows just when—the months of waiting must have seemed endless. This was long before telephone, cable, or radio, and letters from abroad took weeks to arrive.

Many people from the north have the urge to travel to sunny, colorful, tropical lands. Winslow Homer, a reserved Yankee who had his home and studio on the rocky coast of Maine, became far more relaxed when he visited the Bahamas. The watercolors he painted there from the 1880s on have a freshness and sparkle he never equaled in his oils. In "Palm Tree, Nassau," Homer captured the intense blue of the Caribbean and, in the flapping palm fronds, the sensation of the wind. Similarly, the chorus of the song with its "Bring back, bring back..." has the bounding rhythm of a sailing ship moving joyously over the waves as it journeys homeward.

Palm Tree, Nassau. Winslow Homer, American, 1836–1910. Watercolor, 1898.

Moderately fast

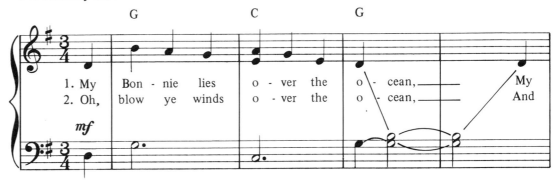

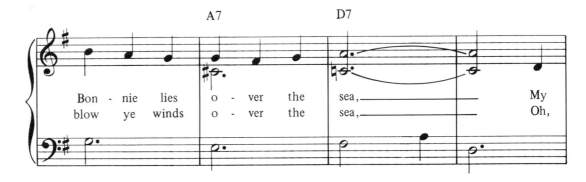

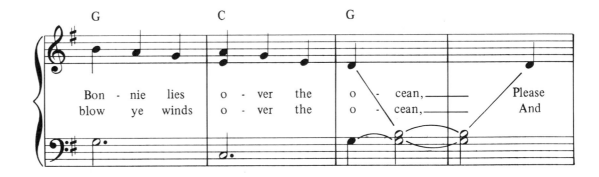

(Please turn the page.)

MY BONNIE LIES OVER THE OCEAN (Continued)

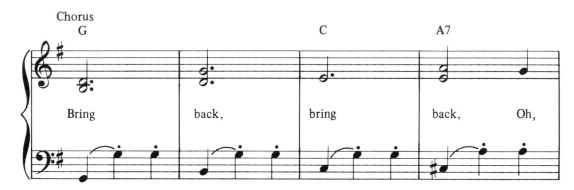

Chorus

Bring back, bring back, Oh,

bring back my Bon - nie to me, to me.

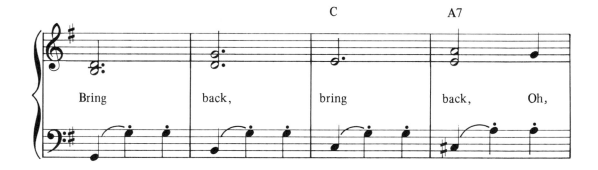

Bring back, bring back, Oh,

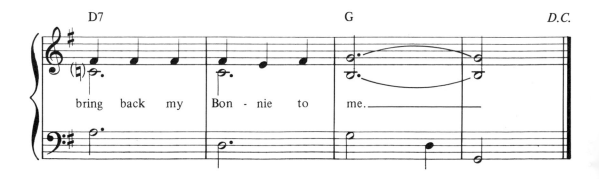

bring back my Bon - nie to me.

Pablo Picasso's print is not realistic like the Homer watercolor, but the young woman has a sad, wistful quality that suggests she may be daydreaming, perhaps of someone far away.

Woman Leaning on Her Elbows.
Pablo Picasso, Spanish, 1881–1973.
Linoleum cut printed in black and light blue-gray inks, 1959.

NOBODY KNOWS THE TROUBLE I'VE SEEN

The American artist Thomas Hart Benton chose rural themes for many of his pictures, showing both blacks and whites hard at work picking cotton, cutting hay, or doing other field work. In "July Hay," he has painted the men working with the eye of a traveler passing through the countryside, treating them as part of the rhythm of the composition rather than as individual people. An artist more sympathetic to the drudgery of hard labor might have seen them quite differently, more in the mood of this very moving spiritual.

July Hay (detail). Thomas Hart Benton, American, 1889–1975. Egg tempera, methyl cellulose, and oil on Masonite, 1943.

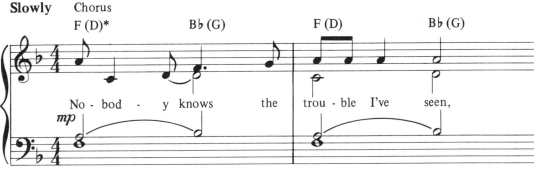

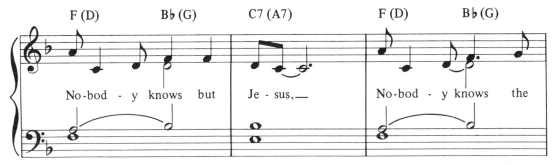

*Guitar: Capo 3rd fret

(Please turn the page.)

NOBODY KNOWS THE TROUBLE I'VE SEEN *(Continued)*

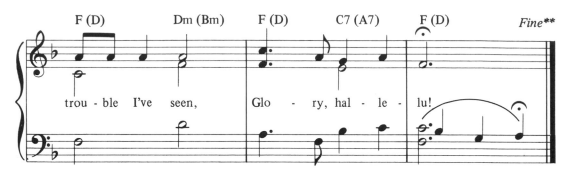

trou - ble I've seen, Glo - ry, hal - le - lu!

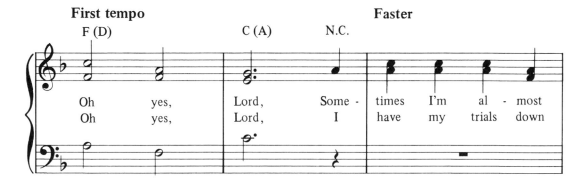

1. Some - times I'm up, some - times I'm down,
2. Al - though you see me goin' 'long so,

Oh yes, Lord, Some - times I'm al - most
Oh yes, Lord, I have my trials down

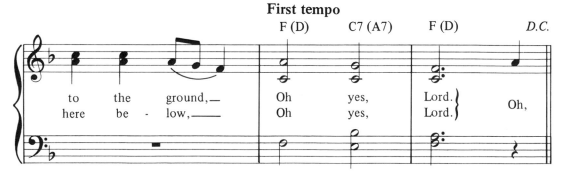

to the ground,— Oh yes, Lord.
here be - low,— Oh yes, Lord. Oh,

**Last time, end here

Although Vincent van Gogh came from a middle-class family, he had a profound feeling for the harsh life of the peasants and working people in his native Holland and later in the South of France. He found beauty in the homely gesture of a woman with work-worn hands cooking pancakes, and he compared his own efforts to achieve truth in his art to those of a peasant toiling in the fields to make things grow.

Peasant Woman Seated by a Fireplace.
Vincent van Gogh, Dutch, 1853–1890.
Oil on canvas.

NOW THE DAY IS OVER

Many poets and artists have been drawn to the twilight hours, when shadows deepen and all is quiet after the bustle of the day. This song is a gentle prayer at nightfall. In his haunting study of a summer evening on Long Island Sound, the painter John F. Kensett created a mood of quiet meditation. Many painters of the time tried to make their landscapes more romantic and picturesque through the use of dramatic lighting or other effects. Kensett, however, gave the scene a quiet, poetic feeling. Using a limited range of colors and a simple composition, he stressed the low horizon and the dark shapes of the island shore silhouetted against the stillness of the sky and water. Even when painting daylight scenes, Kensett avoided brilliant colors, and here the mellow tones of orange, crimson, and gold convey with great sensitivity the fading glow of the setting sun when "night is drawing nigh."

Quietly, not too slow

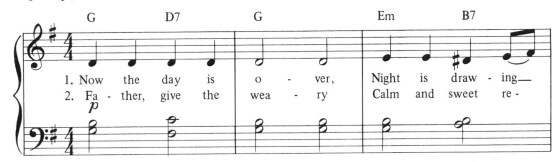

1. Now the day is o - ver, Night is draw - ing
2. Fa - ther, give the wea - ry Calm and sweet re -

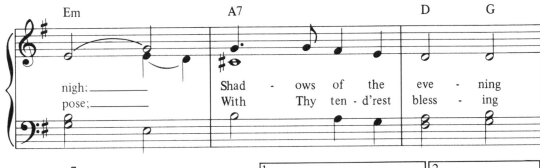

nigh;_____ Shad - ows of the eve - ning
pose;_____ With Thy ten - d'rest bless - ing

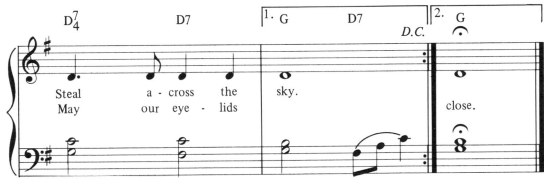

Steal a - cross the sky.
May our eye - lids close.

Twilight on the Sound, Darien, Connecticut (detail). John Frederick Kensett, American, 1816–1872. Oil on canvas, 1872.

This song has the vigorous rhythm of a folk dance, and we can almost hear the clapping of hands and the stomping of feet. With all their consonants, the opening words are quite a tongue twister when sung very fast. John Steuart Curry was one of a group of artists known as Regionalists who painted scenes of rural America. Many of his pictures are of his native Kansas, but this spacious landscape celebrates the prosperous farm country of Wisconsin, where all the crops mentioned in the song grow in abundance. Although the scene is happy and peaceful, there is drama in the contrast between the streaks of sunlight and the dark clouds with their threat of rain. Curry grew up on a farm and was thoroughly familiar with sudden changes of weather. But no matter how intimately one knows country life, there is always, as the song suggests, a mystery and wonder about things that grow in the soil.

OATS, PEAS, AND BEANS

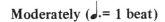

Moderately (♩.= 1 beat)

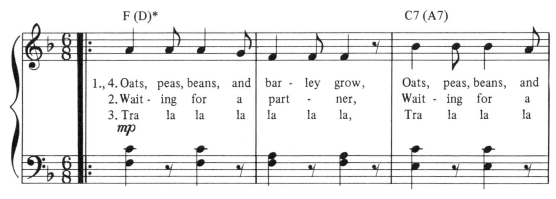

1., 4. Oats, peas, beans, and bar - ley grow,
2. Wait - ing for a part - ner,
3. Tra la la la la la la,

Oats, peas, beans, and
Wait - ing for a
Tra la la la

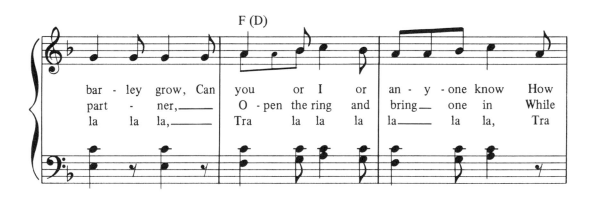

bar - ley grow, Can
part - ner,_____ O
la la la,_____ Tra

you or I or
- pen the ring and
la la la la

an - y -one know How
bring__ one in While
la__ la la, Tra

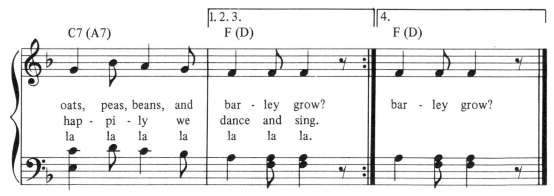

oats, peas, beans, and
hap - pi - ly we
la la la la

bar - ley grow?
dance and sing.
la la la.

bar - ley grow?

*Guitar: Capo 3rd fret

Wisconsin Landscape (detail). John Steuart Curry, American, 1897-1946. Oil on canvas, 1938-39.

OH, DEAR, WHAT CAN THE MATTER BE?

Both the picture on the opposite page and the ever-popular song are about waiting. The painting is called "Penelope," after the faithful wife in the Greek epic tale *The Odyssey* who remained true to her husband Odysseus during his twenty-year absence, despite suitors who tried to persuade her that he would never return. This Penelope, however, is no classical heroine. She is a young lady of the artist's own time, dressed in Renaissance-style costume, doing needlework, and gazing dreamily at a miniature of her absent husband.

This lighthearted song was first heard in Scotland more than two hundred years ago and reminds us that the country fair was a big social event, with much entertainment and with ribbons, toys, trinkets, and all kinds of novelties for sale. The lass in the song loves pretty things to wear and anxiously hopes she can trust her Johnny to remember his many promises and not tarry much longer amid all the fun of the fair.

Yellow Basket of Flowers. American, second quarter 19th century. Watercolor.

Lively (each measure = 1 beat)

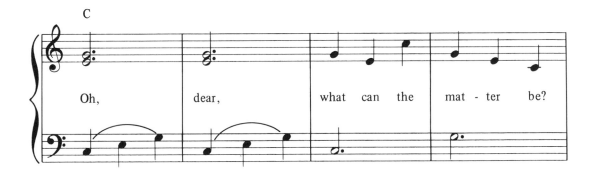

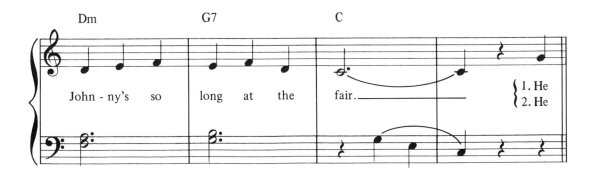

94

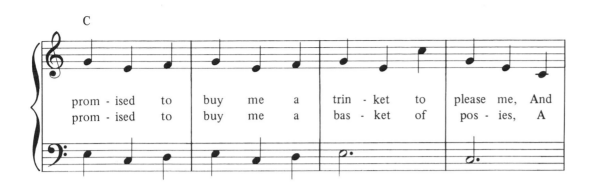

C

prom - ised   to   buy   me   a   trin - ket   to   please   me,   And
prom - ised   to   buy   me   a   bas - ket   of   pos - ies,   A

G7

then   for   a   smile,   oh.   he   vowed   he   would   tease   me,   He
gar - land   of   lil - ies.   a   gift   of   red   ros - es,   A

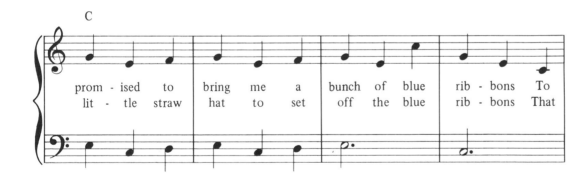

C

prom - ised   to   bring   me   a   bunch   of   blue   rib - bons   To
lit - tle   straw   hat   to   set   off   the   blue   rib - bons   That

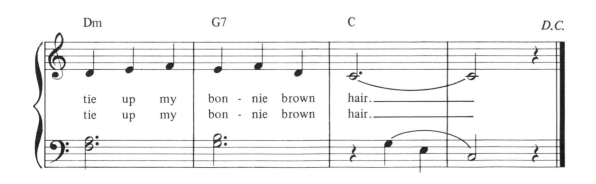

Dm   G7   C   D.C.

tie   up   my   bon - nie   brown   hair.____
tie   up   my   bon - nie   brown   hair.____

Penelope (detail). Charles François Marchal,
French, 1825–1877. Oil on canvas.

95

OH, HOW LOVELY IS THE EVENING

Both the song and William Morris Hunt's painting evoke the magical mood of evening, when the light is fading, shadows lengthen, and trees, bushes, and other forms in nature seem to blend into each other. The song does this through sound. It is a round, sung by several people, with each voice entering in turn, overlapping the preceding voice, then going back to the beginning on reaching the end. The ding-dong refrain of the church bells makes this round especially effective.

William Morris Hunt had studied in Paris and was much influenced by the great landscape painter, Camille Corot. Hunt painted the sand bank and willow trees in Magnolia, Massachusetts, in broad, soft masses with very little color, almost like a charcoal drawing. The edges are blurred, and the small figures of the boy and the little girl become dark silhouettes gazing at the distant lake lit by the last faint glimmer of the setting sun.

Sand Bank with Willows, Magnolia (detail). William Morris Hunt, American, 1824–1879. Oil on canvas, 1877.

Gently flowing

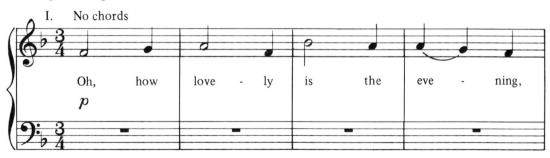

Oh, how love - ly is the eve - ning,

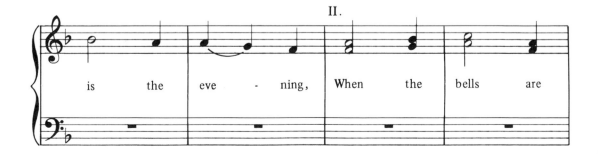

is the eve - ning, When the bells are

The Japanese artist Suzuki Harunobu is noted for his subtle color, flat linear patterns, and exquisite sense of design. In this woodcut, he conveys with simplicity and grace the romantic mood of a young woman on her balcony casting the light of a lantern upward as she gazes at the plum blossoms, scattered like stars against the night sky.

To complete the round, sing or play the left hand alone at III.

OH! SUSANNA

This happy-go-lucky song is popular not only in the South but all over America. It was written by Stephen Foster, and quickly became the anthem of the Gold Rush. The song has the jolly feeling of someone setting out on the open road singing and strumming on a banjo or guitar, and it would naturally appeal to cowboys.

A hundred years ago, an American painter from Philadelphia, Thomas Eakins, spent some time studying cowboy life in the Bad Lands of Dakota. He lived on a ranch, rode a little brown Indian pony called Baldy, and even dressed like the cowboy in the painting. He wore a buckskin coat and fringed pants, a broad-brimmed hat, a colorful neckcloth, and a cartridge belt with a pistol in a holster. Several years later, back in Philadelphia, he had his friend Franklin Schenck pose for him indoors on a green kitchen chair. Schenck could play the banjo and guitar and, dressed in the artist's buckskin outfit, sang the cowboy songs Eakins had enjoyed out West. Although Schenck was not a real cowboy, he looked the part with his full hair and shaggy beard. Eakins was a realist, and he would have found the cowboys in today's movie Westerns much too trim and neat!

Cowboy Singing (detail). Thomas Eakins, American, 1844–1916. Watercolor, ca. 1890.

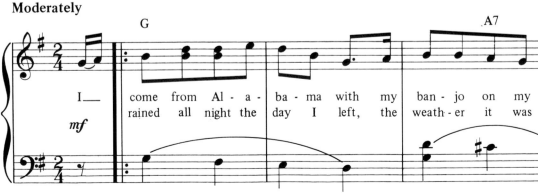

Moderately

I____
come from Al - a - ba - ma with my ban - jo on my
rained all night the day I left, the weath - er it was

knee, I'm_ goin' to Lou - 'si - an - a, my_ true love for to see.
dry, The_ sun so hot I froze to death, Su - san - na don't you cry._

It_

Chorus

Oh! Su - san - na, Oh, don't you cry for me. I've_ come from Al - a - ba - ma with my ban - jo on my knee._

Cowboy at B. T. Ranch, North Dakota (detail). Thomas Eakins, American, 1844–1916. Gelatin-silver print.

Cows. Dutch, Delft, 18th century. Tin-glazed earthenware with polychrome enamels.

Wild Ducks in the Snow (detail). Andō Hiroshige, Japanese, 1797–1858. Woodblock print.

Children love to imitate animal sounds, and this song, with its many verses, gives them a chance to moo like a cow, quack like a duck, and so on. The charming pottery cows from Delft in Holland are playful like the song, and the artist who painted the bright red, green, yellow, and blue designs on them obviously enjoyed himself. In the print of wild ducks the great Japanese artist Hiroshige has created a beautiful landscape that captures the feeling of the first snowfall in winter.

OLD MACDONALD

With spirit

Old Mac-Don-ald had a farm, E - I - E - I - O. And

on this farm he had some {sheep, cows,} E - I - E - I - O. With a

1. baa - baa here and a baa - baa there,
2. moo - moo here and a moo - moo there,

Repeat as necessary, then D.C.

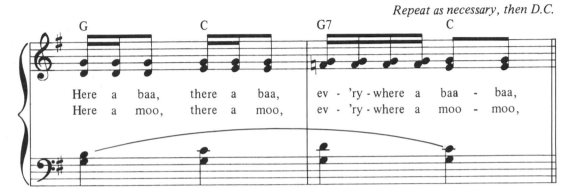

Here a baa, there a baa, ev - 'ry - where a baa - baa,
Here a moo, there a moo, ev - 'ry - where a moo - moo,

Continue in the same manner with chicks...chick, chick; ducks... quack, quack; donkeys...hee haw; dogs...bark, bark; cats...meow; pigs...oink, oink; etc.

Using flat color and just a few lines, the French artist Lucien Laforge depicted a herd of pigs being led to market. In the detail from a Chinese scroll, we can almost hear the clucking of the hen with her chicks as she pecks on the ground in search of tidbits.

Marché (detail). Illustration from an alphabet book by Lucien Laforge, French. Color woodcut, early 20th century. Paris: Henry Goulet.

Hen and chickens. Detail of a handscroll. Chinese, Early Ming Dynasty, 15th century. Colors on silk.

Even when the words and music of a song are sad, we can enjoy singing it or listening to it, and sometimes the sight of a beautiful place we visited long ago brings back memories and gives us comfort. In "On Top of Old Smokey," the singer recalls a time when he and the one he loved were walking together high up on a snowy mountain. He now feels that if he had

been less timid, she would never have left him for someone else and made him so unhappy. The painting by Jerome Thompson of a party of six young people at sunset on a mountainside in western Vermont shares the tender, wistful mood of the song. Some are admiring the dramatic scenery, others are chatting pleasantly, and one hopes that unlike the couple in the

song, they will all remain friends. Jerome Thompson was chiefly known as an illustrator, and only recently have his fine, poetic landscapes come to be appreciated.

The Belated Party on Mansfield Mountain
(detail). Jerome Thompson, American,
1814–1886. Oil on canvas, 1858.

ON TOP OF OLD SMOKEY

Rather quickly

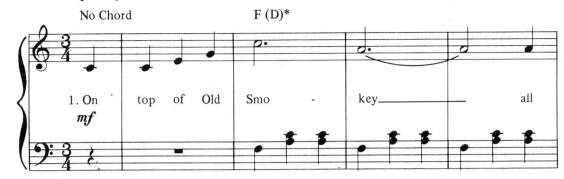

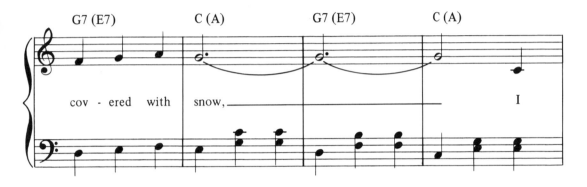

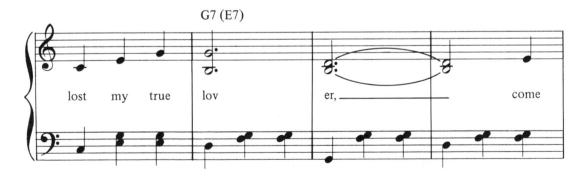

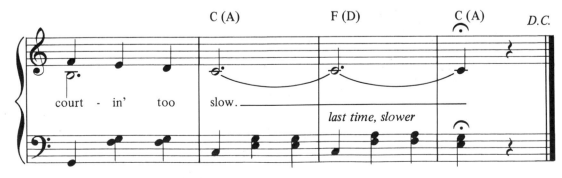

*Guitar: Capo 3rd fret

Additional verses:

2.
For courtin's a pleasure,
    but parting is grief,
And a falsehearted lover
    is worse than a thief.

3.
For a thief, he will rob you
    and take what you have,
But a falsehearted lover will
    send you to your grave.

4.
She'll (he'll) hug you and kiss
    you and tell you more lies
Than the crossties on the railroad
    or the stars in the skies.

5.
On top of Old Smokey all
    covered with snow,
I lost my true lover,
    come courtin' too slow.

POLLY, PUT THE KETTLE ON

Tea time is usually a happy occasion, a chance to relax with family and friends, especially in England. But this little girl, who is about to give her dolls a tea party, looks so cross that she seems determined not to enjoy anything. The self-taught artist who painted this picture used no perspective, and everything, including the tiles, is made to appear flat. The little girl herself looks rather like a stuffed doll. Long ago, children were dressed very elaborately, even in the summertime. The kitten looks more contented than its mistress: A cat in a good home always knows how to relax and enjoy life.

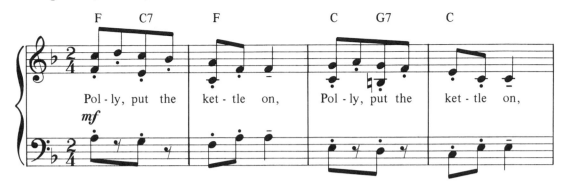

Kettle on stand. From a seven-piece Rococo Revival tea set. William Forbes, American, active 1828–1850. Silver.

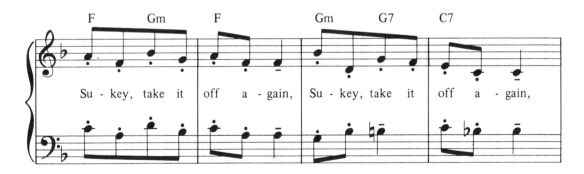

Little Girl with Miniature Tea Set. American, 19th century. Oil on canvas.

POP!
GOES THE
WEASEL

The thought of a mischievous monkey chasing a weasel, whether around a mulberry bush or, in another version, a cobbler's bench, is most entertaining. Both animals can run very fast, and many have long tails, like the sleek, elegant weasel in the Japanese scroll painting on the opposite page. The song evokes a household that remains cheerful in spite of measles and the whooping cough, and a simpler world, long ago, when a needle and a spool of thread cost only a penny each.

Briskly (♩.= 1 beat)

1. All a-round the mul-ber-ry bush the mon-key chased the
2. Ru-fus has the whoop-ing cough, poor Sal-ly has the

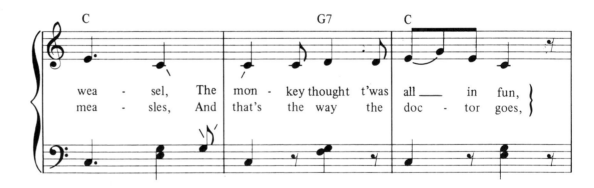

wea-sel, The mon-key thought t'was all ___ in fun,
mea-sles, And that's the way the doc-tor goes,

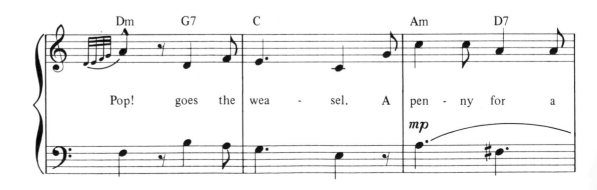

Pop! goes the wea-sel. A pen-ny for a

Jack-in-the-box. Edward Gordon Craig, British, 1872–1966. Hand-colored woodcut from *Gordon Craig's Book of Penny Toys*. London: Lemley & Co., 1899.

106

spool_ of thread, A pen - ny for_ a nee - dle,

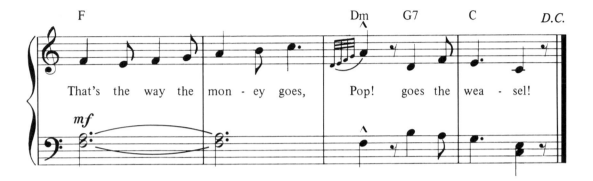

That's the way the mon - ey goes, Pop! goes the wea - sel!

Kantharos (two-handled cup) with monkey's face. Cypriot, probably early 5th century B.C. Painted clay.

Weasel. Detail of a handscroll. Kawanabe Kyōsai, Japanese, 1831–1889. Wash drawing.

RED RIVER VALLEY

Both this song and this painting suggest a bygone era. The title of the song refers to the Red River of the north, which flows through Manitoba in Canada, then between North Dakota and Minnesota. The gentle, wistful melody and words suggest that the young girl's sweetheart is leaving on a long journey. He would probably carry with him a photograph of his loved one and perhaps some other mementos as reminders of the happy hours they spent together.

A photograph is one of the objects that the largely self-taught artist John Frederick Peto depicted in his still-life composition "Old Souvenirs." In it, the canvas is made to look like an office board. The various items, all of which had a special meaning for Peto, seem to be stuck on a rack or pinned directly to the board; they are painted so convincingly that they look real. This style is known as trompe l'oeil, which in French means "to fool the eye."

Old Souvenirs. John Frederick Peto, American, 1854–1907. Oil on canvas, ca. 1881–1900.

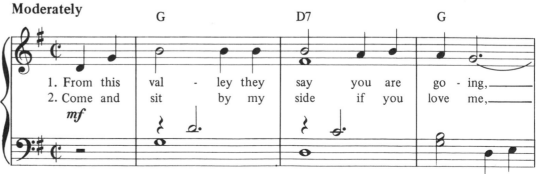

Moderately

G   D7   G

mf

1. From this val - ley they say you are go - ing,____
2. Come and sit by my side if you love me,____

108

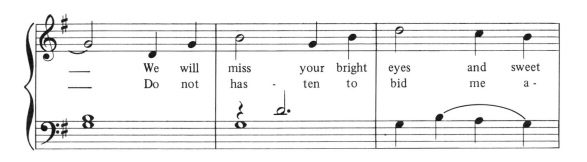

We will miss your bright eyes and sweet
Do not has - ten to bid me a-

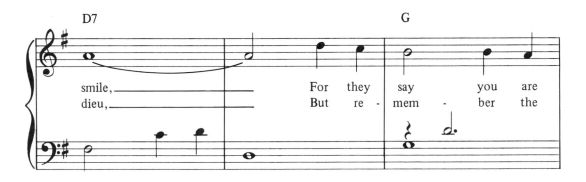

D7   G

smile, _____ For they say you are
dieu, _____ But re - mem - ber the

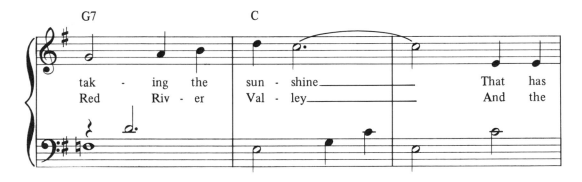

G7   C

tak - ing the sun - shine _____ That has
Red Riv - er Val - ley _____ And the

D7   G   C   G   D.C.

bright - ened our path - way a while. _____
girl that has loved you so true. _____

Rummaging through a drawer or an attic we often come across such odds and ends as an old envelope, a train ticket, a newspaper clipping, or a theater program, which can bring back experiences of long ago. This is what Peto has done in his painting on which he worked, off and on, for almost twenty years. The folded copy of the *Philadelphia Evening Bulletin* is dated October 10, 1881, when the picture was probably begun. The "photo" of the artist's little daughter Helena, age about seven, was added some nineteen years later, painted over an earlier portrait. Other items include an upside-down postcard addressed to Peto and a greeting card decorated with a lily. In spite of the realistic treatment, the effect is not photographic, and the picture's design gives it quite a modern look.

The Last To Go. Randolph Caldecott, British, 1846–1886. Color illustration from *Gleanings from the "Graphic."* London: George Routledge and Sons, 1889.

THE RIDDLE SONG

In this painting by the Florentine artist Fra Filippo Lippi, it at first looks as if the gentleman poking his head through the window is courting the richly dressed woman and offering her a love token. But this is not, as it was once thought to be, a betrothal or a wedding picture. The embroidered coat of arms in the man's left hand is that of the noble Scolari family of Florence. Historians now believe that this couple had been married for several years when the picture was painted and that it celebrates the birth of their first child, a boy named Ranieri.

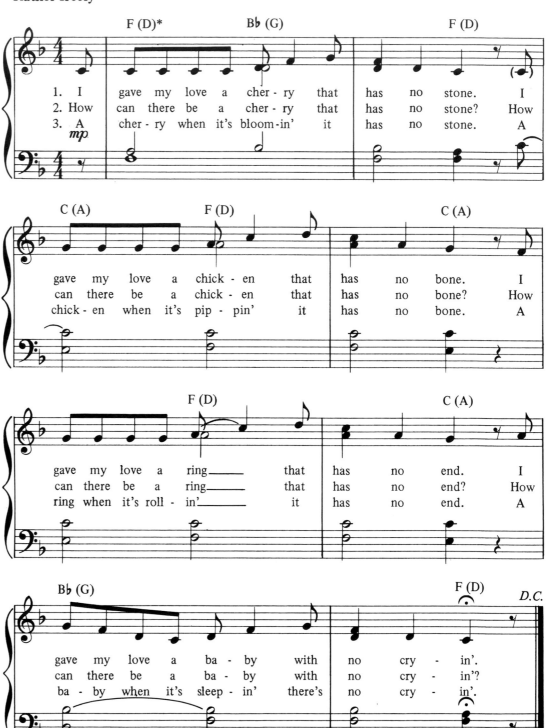

Rather freely

F (D)*   Bb (G)   F (D)

1. I gave my love a cher-ry that has no stone. I
2. How can there be a cher-ry that has no stone? How
3. A cher-ry when it's bloom-in' it has no stone. A

mp

C (A)   F (D)   C (A)

gave my love a chick-en that has no bone. I
can there be a chick-en that has no bone? How
chick-en when it's pip-pin' it has no bone. A

F (D)   C (A)

gave my love a ring_____ that has no end. I
can there be a ring_____ that has no end? How
ring when it's roll-in'_____ it has no end. A

Bb (G)   F (D)   D.C.

gave my love a ba-by with no cry-in'.
can there be a ba-by with no cry-in'?
ba-by when it's sleep-in' there's no cry-in'.

*Guitar: capo 3rd fret

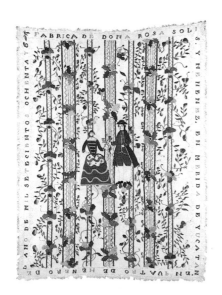

Wedding bedspread. Dona Rosa Solis y Menenez, Mexican (Yucatán). Colored silks on weft-ribbed cotton ground, 1786.

Portrait of a Man and Woman at a Casement. Fra Filippo Lippi, Italian, ca. 1406–1469. Tempera on wood.

ROCK-A-BYE, BABY

Mothers the world over have rocked their babies to sleep with soothing lullabies, and in Britain and America this is the best known of them all, sung in thousands of homes at nightfall. The origins of the rhyme and melody are uncertain. It is believed that long ago cradles were rocked by wind power. The cradle falling is not as alarming as it may seem, for the gentle rhythm of the song suggests a baby sinking slowly, peacefully into slumberland. In both the stone carving by the Eskimo artist Oshaweektuk-A of a mother holding her baby and the print "Mother's Kiss" by the American artist Mary Cassatt, the warm, tender emotion is the same.

Mother's Kiss (detail). Mary Cassatt, American, 1844–1926. Drypoint and aquatint, ca. 1891.

Mother and Child. Oshaweektuk-A, Canadian. Made at Cape Dorset, Northwest Territories. Stone, 1956.

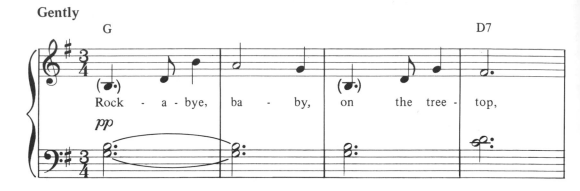

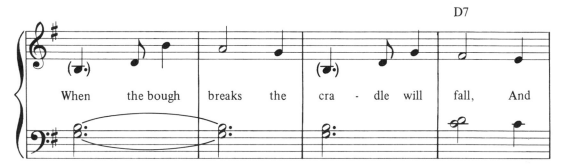

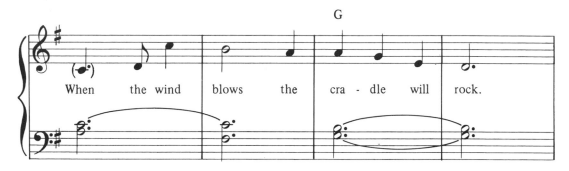

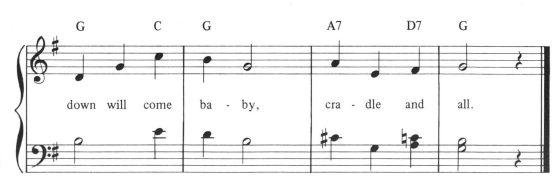

113

SCARBOROUGH FAIR

A Dance in the Country (detail).
Giovanni Domenico Tiepolo, Italian,
1727–1804. Oil on canvas, ca. 1756.

Detail of an embroidered box. English, third
quarter 17th century. Silk, satin, and metal
threads, with seed pearls and coral.

Moderately flowing

1. Are you go - ing to Scar - bor - ough Fair? Sing
2. Tell her to buy me an a - cre of land, Sing

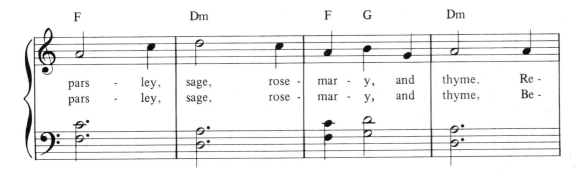

F		Dm		F	G	Dm	

pars - ley, sage, rose - mar - y, and thyme. Re -
pars - ley, sage, rose - mar - y, and thyme, Be -

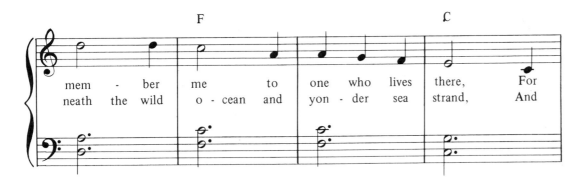

mem - ber me to one who lives there, For
neath the wild o - cean and yon - der sea strand, And

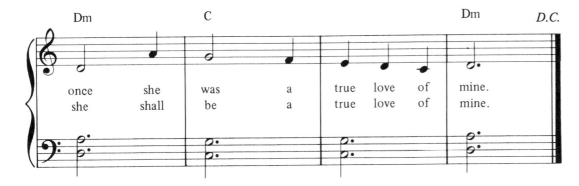

once she was a true love of mine.
she shall be a true love of mine.

Additional verses:

3.
Tell her to make me a cambric shirt,
Sing parsley, sage, rosemary, and thyme,
Without any stitching or needlework,
And she shall be a true love of mine.

4.
Tell her to wash it in yonder dry well,
Sing parsley, sage, rosemary, and thyme,
Where water ne'er sprung
    nor a drop of rain fell,
And she shall be a true love of mine.

5.
Tell her to dry it on yonder sharp thorn,
Sing parsley, sage, rosemary, and thyme,
Which never bore blossom
    since Adam was born,
And she shall be a true love of mine.

This song refers to a real seaside place, Scarborough, in northern England. Beginning in the Middle Ages, a yearly fair was held there by royal decree. At first it took place on the sands, on "yonder sea strand," but by the time the song was written it had moved into the town. Fairs were originally held to mark religious holidays, but there was much merry-making and entertainment at them, too.

In "A Dance in the Country," the Venetian painter Giovanni Domenico Tiepolo has pictured a lively dance in the garden of one of the country villas where people of fashion spent the summer. The painting has some of the lilting rhythm and poetic mood of the song. The dancers and other people in the painting are members of the *commedia dell'arte,* a troupe of actors popular in Italy from the sixteenth through the eighteenth centuries. Venetians loved to dress up in the colorful costumes of the Harle-quin and other characters from the *commedia.* On all important religious and civic holidays, they were allowed to wear masks, even maids going to market and mothers nursing their babies, who also wore tiny masks!

The spirited, bouncing rhythm of this song evokes the robust hillbilly world of hoedowns and square dances. We can picture the excitement in a small country town when the stagecoach or the old "iron horse" was due to arrive. There must have been a special thrill in the first sight of the sturdy horses rounding the bend on the mountainside pulling the lumbering coach, or of the puffing locomotive with its cowcatcher followed by the long string of cars on the winding track. People would rush out to greet the coach or train, some in order to meet long-awaited friends and relatives or to pick up mail, others just for the fun of the occasion —a welcome break in the daily routine. The charming little color woodcut at the right by the French artist Lucien Laforge of a coach and white horses scaling an impossibly steep and very stylized hill is an illustration from an alphabet book. The striking French poster design of 1929 on the opposite page uses the sleek shape of the powerful locomotive as a symbol of absolute accuracy and precision. This was a train that was sure to arrive exactly on time!

SHE'LL BE COMIN' 'ROUND THE MOUNTAIN

Fantasmagorie. Illustration from an alphabet book by Lucien Laforge, French. Color woodcut, early 20th century. Paris: Henry Goulet.

Brightly, with spirit

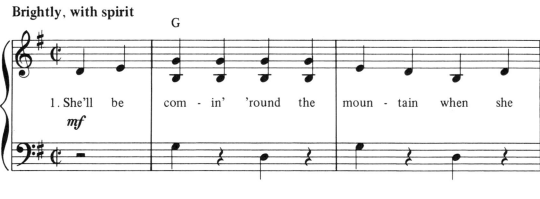

1. She'll be com - in' 'round the moun - tain when she

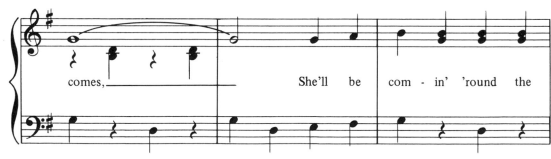

comes, _____ She'll be com - in' 'round the

mountain when she comes, _____ She'll be

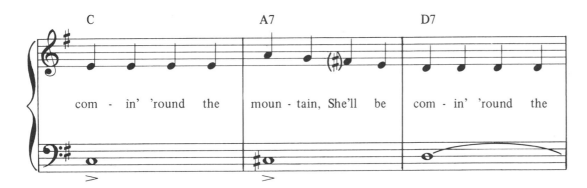

comin' 'round the mountain, she'll be

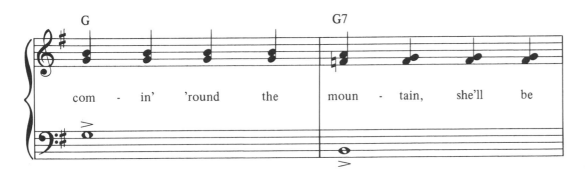

comin' 'round the mountain, She'll be comin' 'round the

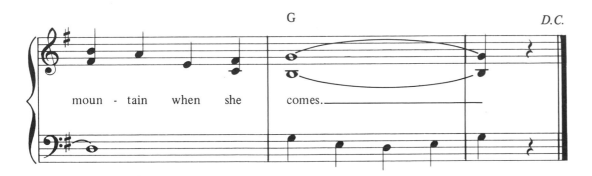

mountain when she comes. _____

Additional verses:

2.
She'll be drivin' six white horses
    when she comes,
She'll be drivin' six white horses
    when she comes,
She'll be drivin' six white horses,
She'll be drivin' six white horses,
She'll be comin' 'round the
    mountain when she comes.

3.
Oh, we'll all come out to greet her
    when she comes,
Yes, we'll all come out to greet her
    when she comes,
Oh, we'll all come out to greet her,
Yes, we'll all come out to meet her,
She'll be comin' 'round the
    mountain when she comes.

Exactitude. Pierre Fix-Masseau, French, b. 1905. Gouache, after a poster of 1929.

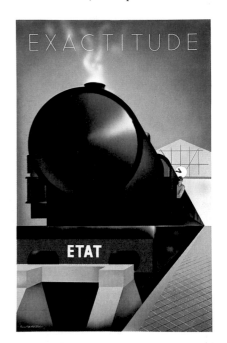

Fur Traders Descending the Missouri.
George Caleb Bingham, American,
1808–1879. Oil on canvas, ca. 1845.

SHENANDOAH

Both the beautiful song "Shenandoah" and George Caleb Bingham's haunting picture "Fur Traders Descending the Missouri" capture the wonder and majesty of America's great rivers. They remind us of a time when there were still vast territories left to explore before railroads and modern industry changed the country. Shenandoah is the name of a river and a valley in Virginia, but in the song it becomes a person. The singer's love for Shenandoah's daughter, whom he must leave to cross "the wide Missouri," makes the subject all the more romantic.

Bingham was born in Virginia, and as a boy moved with his family to Missouri. He painted many scenes of river life in the Midwest, but this is his masterpiece. The artist understood the hard life of the fur traders. The old man steering the canoe has a wary, suspicious look, and his son, sprawled on the cargo, is daydreaming. We are fascinated, too, by the mysterious silhouette of the pet fox. The figures in the boat are sharp and clear, contrasting wonderfully with the hazy but luminous atmosphere and the glassy stillness of the water.

119

Peaceable Kingdom.
Edward Hicks,
American, 1780–1849.
Oil on canvas,
ca. 1830.

The Quakers, who prefer to be called Friends, belong to a branch of Christianity that believes in brotherhood, nonviolence, truthfulness, and a quiet, modest way of life. Another group, the Shakers, hold many of the same views. This old Shaker hymn expresses the belief that to be pure in heart and true to oneself, or "simple" as the Shakers would say, is the greatest gift.

Edward Hicks, a completely self-taught artist, was a Quaker from Pennsylvania who painted several pictures of an ideal place, which he called the "Peaceable Kingdom." He depicted a happy state prophesied by Isaiah in the Old Testament where "The wolf also shall dwell with the lamb. . .and a little child shall lead them."

SIMPLE GIFTS

Moderately

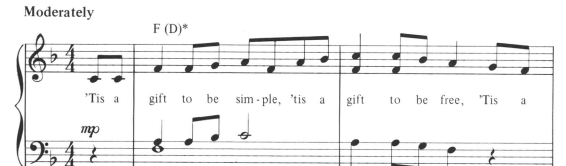

F (D)*

'Tis a gift to be sim-ple, 'tis a gift to be free, 'Tis a

C7 (A7)

gift to come down to where we ought to be, And

F (D)

when we find our-selves in the place just right, 'Twill

*Guitar: Capo 3rd fret

(Please turn the page.)

ISAIAH 11 Chap 576

SIMPLE GIFTS *(Continued)*

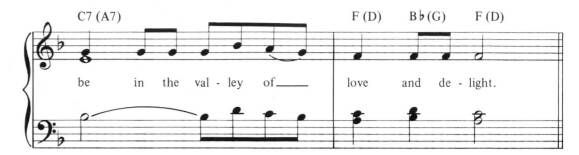

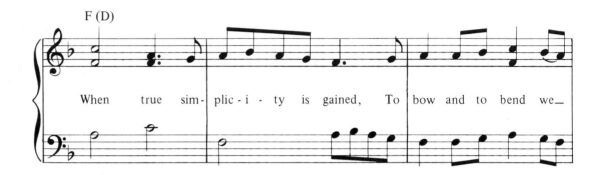

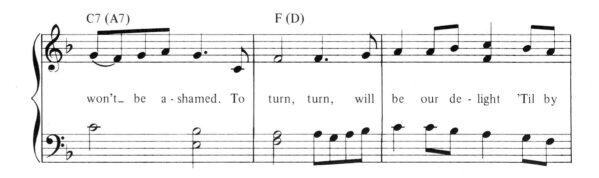

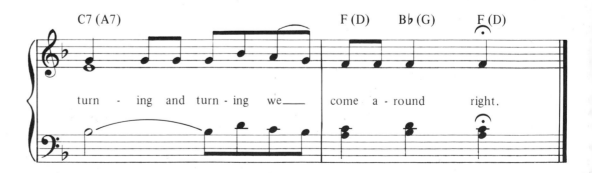

Although the Shakers' way of life would be too severe for most people today, their furniture is much admired by modern designers for its spare simplicity, its purity of line, its flawless craftsmanship, and its strong, sensitive handling of wood and metal. The walls of many Shaker interiors were lined with pegs on which they could hang chairs, hats, shawls, bonnets, and other objects. The slat-back chair was a typical item of furniture, and the Shakers were probably the first in the United States to produce rocking chairs in quantity, both for their own community and for sale. They even invented the common clothespin.

Corner of a Shaker retiring room from the North family dwelling. American (New Lebanon, New York), 1830–40.

Pies are mentioned in several favorite nursery rhymes, including "Little Jack Horner" and "Sing a Song of Sixpence." Here the pies offered for sale by the pieman on his way to the fair must have looked very tempting to poor Simple Simon. In a third verse that is sometimes sung, Simon goes fishing for a whale but catches only a pail of water, and in a fourth, he foolishly tries to see if plums grow on thistles. When he pricks himself, he whistles instead of crying like a normal boy would do.

The boy in George Luks's painting is no "Simple Simon." He is probably just thinking his own thoughts.

SIMPLE SIMON

Allegretto

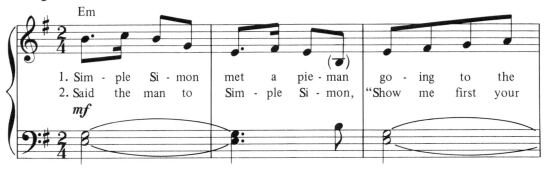

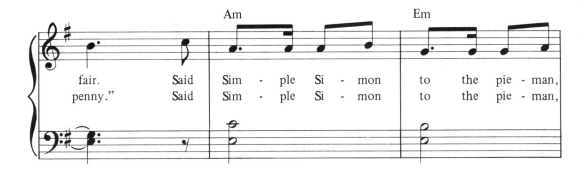

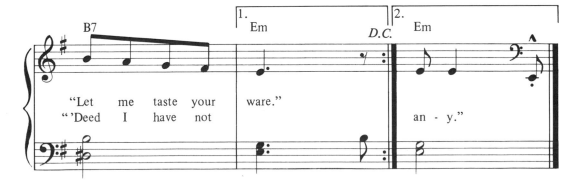

1. Simple Simon met a pieman going to the fair. Said Simple Simon to the pieman, "Let me taste your ware."
2. Said the man to Simple Simon, "Show me first your penny." Said Simple Simon to the pieman, "'Deed I have not any."

Boy with Baseball (detail). George Luks, American, 1867–1933. Oil on canvas, ca. 1925.

The Feast of Ahasuerus (detail). Woodcut, ca. 1480. Originally reproduced in black and white in *Der Spiegel der Menschen Behaltnis.* Speyer: Peter Drach, 1479–1481. Reproduced here with added colors.

SKIP TO MY LOU

Square-dance tempo

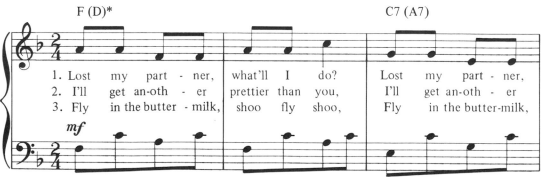

1. Lost my part - ner, what'll I do? Lost my part - ner,
2. I'll get an-oth - er prettier than you, I'll get an-oth - er
3. Fly in the butter - milk, shoo fly shoo, Fly in the butter-milk,

mf

Snap the Whip (detail). Winslow Homer,
American, 1836–1910. Oil on canvas, 1872.

*Guitar: Capo 3rd fret

124

F (D)

what'll I do?
prettier than you,
shoo fly shoo,

Lost my part-ner,
I'll get an-oth-er
Fly in the butter-milk,

what'll I do?
prettier than you,
shoo fly shoo,

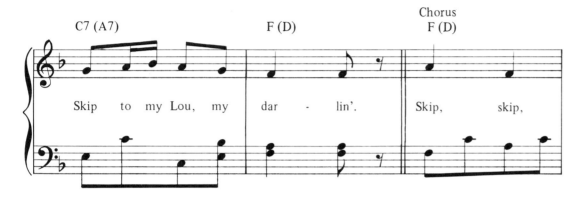

C7 (A7)   F (D)   Chorus
                                F (D)

Skip to my Lou, my   dar - lin'.   Skip,   skip,

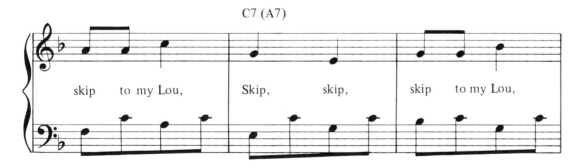

C7 (A7)

skip to my Lou,   Skip,   skip,   skip to my Lou,

F (D)   C7 (A7)   F (D)
                                      D.C.

Skip, skip,   skip to my Lou,   Skip to my Lou, my   dar - lin'.

Many songs in this book are English, but this one, a popular square-dance tune, is as thoroughly American as Winslow Homer's painting. There are several dances to the bouncy tune of "Skip to My Lou." In one version, boys and girls choose partners and form a circle. One boy has no partner, and as he moves around the circle and chooses a girl everyone claps and joins in the singing. The change of partners goes on, and sometimes new verses are made up as the dance continues. "Lou" is an old word for sweetheart, and lines like "fly in the buttermilk" give us amusing glimpses of rural life in pioneer America.

The eight boys playing "Snap the Whip" in Homer's painting remind us of Mark Twain's Tom Sawyer and his friends. In the game, the children join hands and those at the front of the long chain run as fast as they can—the winding movement as they run is like the coiling of a whip—trying to throw off the children at the other end. Both the game and the dance are quite strenuous, and when they are over everyone is exhausted, but happy.

SKYE BOAT SONG

This sad, beautiful song recalls a dramatic episode in Scottish history. Once separate kingdoms, England and Scotland had been united as Great Britain, and in the period referred to in the song, they were ruled by George II, a German-born king of the House of Hanover. Many Scots remained loyal to the House of Stuart, which had ruled Britain in the previous century, even though the last Stuart king, James II, had been so unpopular that he had been forced to flee to France in 1688. In 1745, many Highlanders rose in support of James II's grandson, Charles Edward Stuart, known as "Bonnie Prince Charlie." He was charming and brave and tried to win back the English throne with the aid of Scottish clans. But the rugged Highlanders, wielding broadswords called claymores, were crushingly defeated by the British troops in 1746 at the bloody battle of Culloden. Flora Macdonald helped Charles escape, smuggling the prince, disguised as her maidservant, in an open boat "over the sea to Skye," an island in the Inner Hebrides. How different from his arrival in a splendid sailing ship the year before! Although some loyal supporters still hoped he would come again, Charles fled to France and died years later in Rome.

Ship at Sea (detail). Ludolf Backhuysen, Dutch, 1631–1708. Pen and brown ink with gray wash, over traces of graphite.

Gently, like a boat rocking

Speed, bon-ny boat, like a bird on the wing, On-ward, the sail-ors cry!

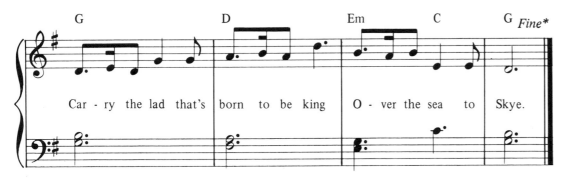

Car-ry the lad that's born to be king O-ver the sea to Skye.

1. Loud the winds howl! Loud the waves roar! Thun-der clouds rend the air!

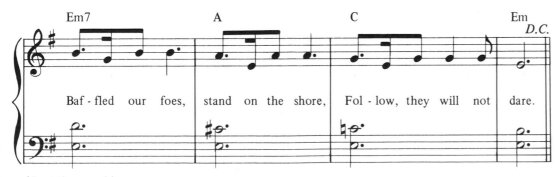

Baf-fled our foes, stand on the shore, Fol-low, they will not dare.

*Last time, end here

D.C.

Additional verses:

2.
Though the waves leap,
   soft shall ye sleep,
Ocean's a royal bed.
Rocked in the deep,
   Flora will keep
Watch by your weary head.
(*Chorus*)

3.
Many's the lad fought
   on that day
Well the claymore could wield.
When the night came,
   silently lay
Dead on Culloden's field.
(*Chorus*)

4.
Burn'd are our homes,
   exile and death
Scatter the loyal men,
Yet, e'er the sword
   cool in the sheath,
Charlie will come again.
(*Chorus*)

Ship pendant. Probably southern European, second half 16th century. Gold, partially enameled, and painted rock crystal, with a pearl.

SWEET BETSY FROM PIKE

This song was a great favorite during the Gold Rush in the middle of the nineteenth century, when thousands of adventurous souls traveled to California, and later to Colorado, to reach the newly discovered gold fields where they hoped to make their fortunes. Among these hopefuls were Sweet Betsy from Pike and her faithful lover, Ike. They had set out in fine style with their two yoke of oxen and other animals, but by the time they reached the desert, poor Betsy was in utter despair, and without Ike's encouragement, their venture would have ended miserably.

Like the family in Frederic M. Grant's romantic painting showing a stalwart young farmer with his wife and baby, alone in a mountain landscape that is relieved only by a humble cottage, Betsy and Ike have few possessions, but they have each other. With the eternal optimism of youth, they know that there will always be tomorrow.

Cock-a-doodle-doo! Walter Crane, British, 1845–1915. Woodcut from *Household Stories* by The Brothers Grimm. London: Macmillan & Co., 1882.

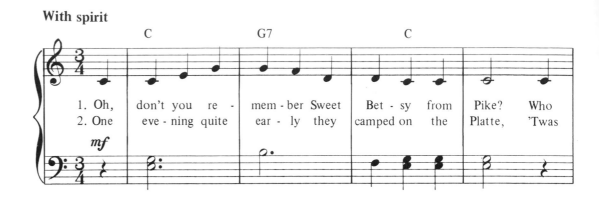

With spirit

1. Oh, don't you re- mem-ber Sweet Bet-sy from Pike? Who
2. One eve-ning quite ear-ly they camped on the Platte, 'Twas

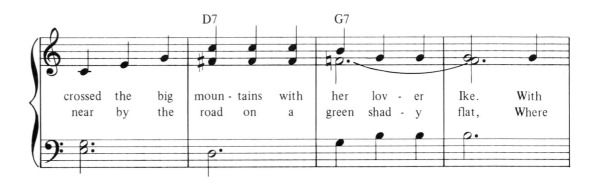

crossed the big moun-tains with her lov-er Ike. With
near by the road on a green shad-y flat, Where

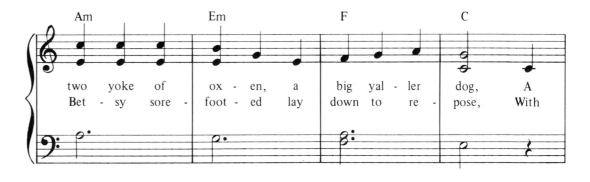

two yoke of ox-en, a big yal-ler dog, A
Bet-sy sore-foot-ed lay down to re-pose, A

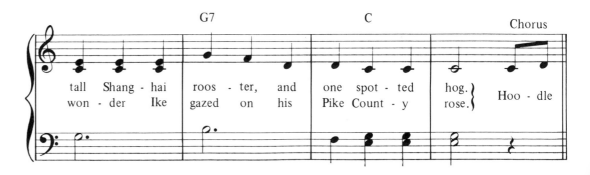

tall Shang-hai roos-ter, and one spot-ted hog.) Hoo-dle
won-der Ike gazed on his Pike Count-y rose.)

Chorus

dang fol - de di - do, hoo - dle dang fol - de day.

Additional verses:

3.
The Shanghai ran off,
    and their cattle all died.
That morning the last piece of
    bacon was fried.
Poor Ike was discouraged
    and Betsy got mad.
The dog drooped his tail and
    looked wondrously sad.
(Chorus)

4.
They soon reached the desert
    where Betsy gave out,
And down in the sand she lay
    rolling about,
While Ike half distracted,
    looked on with surprise,
Saying, "Betsy, get up,
    you'll get sand in your eyes."
(Chorus)

5.
Sweet Betsy got up in a
    great deal of pain,
Declared she'd go back to
    Pike County again;
But Ike gave a sigh,
    and they fondly embraced,
And they traveled along with
    his arm round her waist.
(Chorus)

6.
Repeat first verse and Chorus

The Homestead (detail). Frederic M. Grant,
American, 1886–1959. Oil on canvas. ca. 1933.

THERE WAS AN OLD LADY

Briskly and rather freely

1. There was an old la-dy who swal-lowed a fly, She swal-lowed a fly, I

don't know why; I hope she don't die. 2. There was an old la-dy who

swal-lowed a spi-der That wrig-gled and wig-gled and jig-gled in-side her. She

swal-lowed the spi-der to catch the fly, She swal-lowed the fly, I

(Please turn the page.)

In this song the story gets more and more fantastic, and very funny, as the creatures the old lady swallows get bigger and bigger. The woman in this painting looks very prim and serious as she sits in all her finery holding a white fan, but she obviously liked animals, since she is surrounded by two birds, two butterflies, and a black cat.

The painter, Rufus Hathaway, was a self-taught artist—there were many in early America—who traveled about the countryside looking for people who wanted their pictures painted. This portrait has character and charm, and the lady, Mrs. Molly Leonard, was probably very pleased with it.

Netsuke: Monkey looking at a fly through a magnifying glass. Japanese. Ivory, 19th century.

Lady with Her Pets. Rufus Hathaway, American, 1770(?)–1822. Oil on canvas, 1790.

131

THERE WAS AN OLD LADY *(Continued)*

don't know why; I hope she don't die. 3. There was an old la-dy who

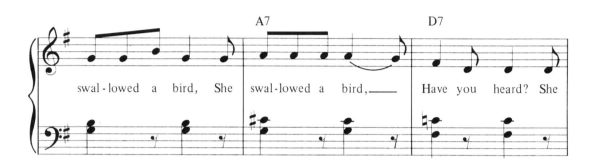

swal-lowed a bird, She swal-lowed a bird,___ Have you heard? She

swal-lowed the bird to catch the spi-der That wrig-gled and wig-gled and

jig-gled in-side her. She swal-lowed the spi-der to catch the fly, She

swal-lowed the fly, I don't know why; I hope she don't die.

A raven, a dog, and a donkey.
Alexander Calder, American, 1898–1976.
Three illustrations from *Fables of Aesop
according to Sir Roger L'Estrange.* Paris:
Harrison, 1931.

Continue in the same manner:

4. There was an old lady who swallowed a cat,
   She swallowed a cat, imagine that!
   She swallowed the cat to catch the bird,
   She swallowed the bird to catch the spider, *etc.*

5. There was an old lady who swallowed a dog,
   She swallowed a dog as big as a hog.
   She swallowed the dog to catch the cat,
   She swallowed the cat to catch the bird,
   She swallowed the bird to catch the spider, *etc.*

6. There was an old lady who swallowed a cow,
   She swallowed a cow, I don't know how.
   She swallowed the cow to catch the dog,
   She swallowed the dog to catch the cat,
   She swallowed the cat to catch the bird,
   She swallowed the bird to catch the spider, *etc.*

7. There was an old lady who swallowed a horse. . .
   (Spoken) She died of course!

THE TREE IN THE WOOD

This is one of those songs in which each verse builds on the one before. Unexpectedly, as the verses get longer the objects and creatures get smaller. We begin with a fine big tree, as solid and as firmly rooted in the ground as the oak in Claude Monet's painting, and we end up with a flea on a feather. Several people take turns singing the verses, and all join in the chorus. The words are playful, but what they say is true, for everything, large or small, is part of nature.

When Monet painted this scene in the forest of Fontainebleau near Paris, he probably did not look at every leaf and branch. He was more interested in the general effect they created than in specific details. Monet knew that colors and shapes look different as the light changes, and that each color affects those around it. As he painted the green of the grass, he thought of the bright patches of sunlight on the ground and the rich deep tones of the tree trunk, and he made the dark branches contrast with the clear blue of the sky.

This song is sung in cumulative fashion like "Green Grow the Rushes-O." After the first verse, sing each additional verse and repeat the earlier ones in reverse order. When you reach the last verse, sing verses 12 to 1 to complete the song.

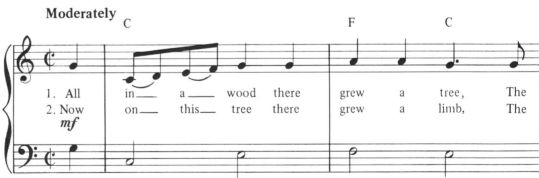

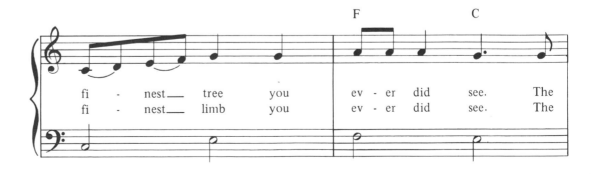

The Bodmer Oak, Fontainebleau Forest.
Claude Monet, French, 1840–1926.
Oil on canvas, ca. 1866.

134

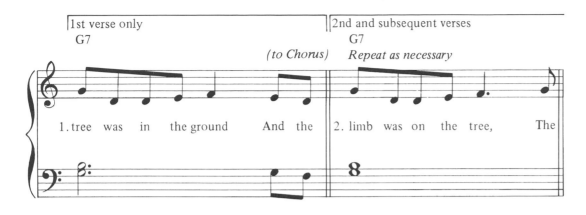

1st verse only
G7
(to Chorus)

2nd and subsequent verses
G7
Repeat as necessary

1. tree was in the ground   And the | 2. limb was on the tree,   The

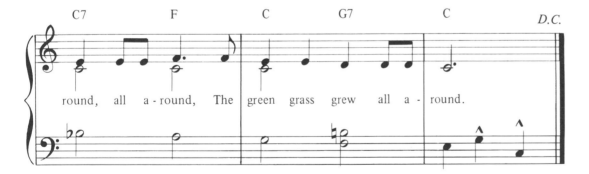

(to Chorus) | Chorus
C   G7

tree was in the ground,   And the | green   grass   grew   all a-

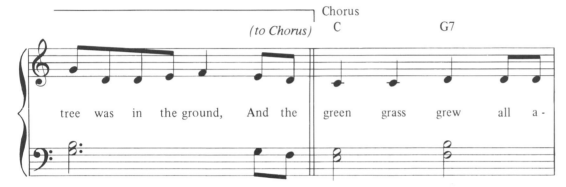

C7   F   C   G7   C   D.C.

round, all a-round, The | green   grass   grew   all a- | round.

Continue similarly:

3.
Now on this limb there grew a branch...

4.
Now on this branch there was a bough...

5.
Now on this bough there was a twig...

6.
And on this twig there was a leaf...

7.
And by this leaf there was a nest...

8.
And in the nest there was an egg...

9.
And in this egg there was a bird...

10.
And on this bird there was a wing...

11.
And on this wing there was a feather...

12.
And on this feather there was a flea...

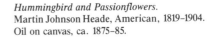
When the American painter Martin Johnson Heade visited Brazil, he chose a tiny hummingbird as the subject for several small paintings, contrasting the bird with the distant landscape and sky. Even though he rendered the bird, the vivid passionflowers, and the lush, tangled vegetation very precisely, he was able to capture at the same time the moist atmosphere and the brilliant light of the exotic tropical scenery.

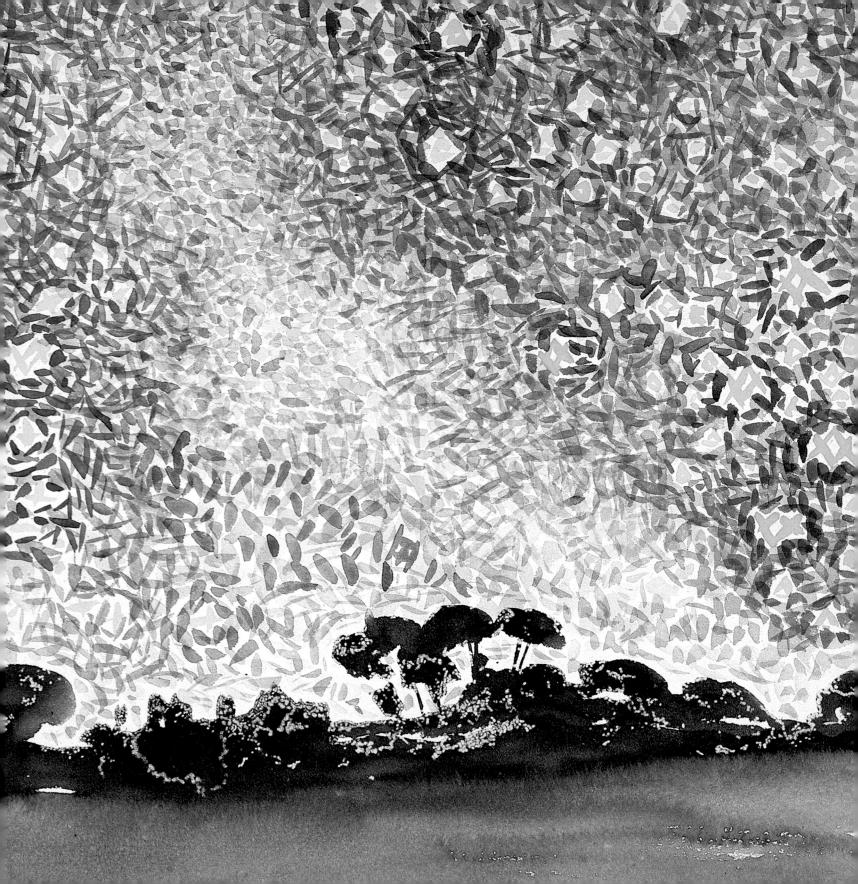

TWINKLE, TWINKLE, LITTLE STAR

There is something magical and mysterious about nighttime, and for thousands of years people have looked up in wonder at the moon and stars. It is not easy to capture the feeling of night in a painting, for we do not see things around us clearly and have to use our imagination. The French artist Henri Edmond Cross, influenced by the Impressionists, painted this country landscape in southern France in watercolor. The trees by the dim water are very low in the picture—we see them as dark silhouettes, faintly touched by moonlight. Most of the space is filled by the night sky, which is really, as we hear in the song, "up above the world so high." Perhaps whoever wrote the words of the song saw only one star twinkling in the sky that night, but here we see dozens, glistening and turning the sky into a lovely magic carpet. By using dabs of paint in a technique sometimes called pointillism and by choosing watercolor, which lets the white of the paper show through, the artist has given the whole scene a wonderful sparkle.

Landscape with Stars (detail). **Henri Edmond Cross, French, 1856–1910. Watercolor.**

Gently, not too slow

1. Twin-kle, twin-kle, lit-tle star,
   When the blaz-ing sun is gone,
   How I won-der
   When he noth-ing
   what you are,
   shines up-on,
   Up a-bove the
   Then you show your
   world so high,
   lit-tle light,
   Like a dia-mond
   Twin-kle, twin-kle
   in the sky.
   all the night.
   Twin-kle, twin-kle,
   lit-tle star,
   How I won-der
   what you are.

*Guitar: Capo 3rd fret

137

WE GATHER TOGETHER

The career of Grandma Moses is an American success story of a very special kind. Born on a farm in Washington County, New York, she led for many years the busy, strenuous life of a farm wife. After her husband died, she started embroidering pictures in worsted yarn.

Moderately

1. We gath - er to - geth - er to ask the Lord's
2. Be - side us to guide us our God with us
3. We all do ex - tol thee, Thou Lead - er tri -

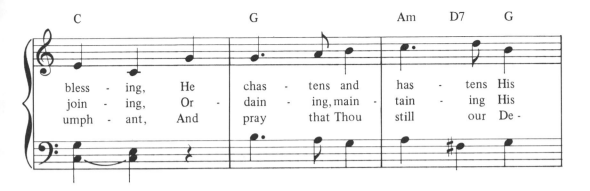

C		G		Am	D7	G

bless - ing, He   chas - tens and   has - tens His
join - ing, Or - dain - ing, main - tain - ing His
umph - ant, And   pray   that Thou   still   our De -

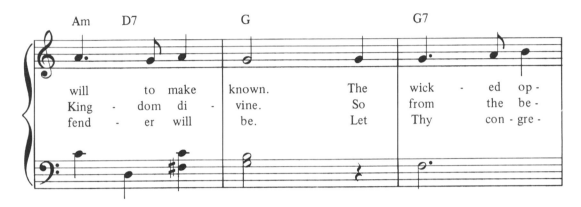

Am	D7	G		G7

will   to make   known.   The   wick - ed op -
King - dom di - vine.   So   from   the be -
fend - er will   be.   Let   Thy   con - gre -

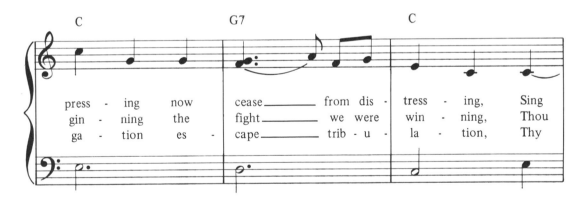

C		G7		C

press - ing now   cease_____ from dis - tress - ing, Sing
gin - ning the   fight_____ we were   win - ning, Thou
ga - tion es -   cape_____ trib - u - la - tion, Thy

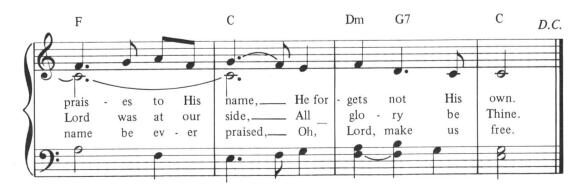

F		C		Dm	G7	C	D.C.

prais - es to His   name,_____ He for - gets not His   own.
Lord was at our   side,_____ All glo - ry be   Thine.
name be ev - er   praised,_____ Oh, Lord, make us   free.

When Grandma Moses was in her seventies, her fingers became too stiff to handle a needle and she began to paint in oil. She never had an art lesson, but knew what she wanted to paint—her early memories of life on the farm. She exhibited her first pictures, along with her preserves, at county fairs. With their cheerful colors and simple yet animated compositions, her paintings recalled a vanished rural America less complicated than the modern world, and they soon reached a wider public, becoming immensely popular. "Thanksgiving Turkey," painted when she was 83—she lived to be 101—is typical of her work. There is a directness and candor, as well as a decorative feeling for pattern, in the placement of the people and turkeys, seen in profile against the snow, and a charming touch of humor in the dog hidden in the tall grass. In all of Grandma Moses's work there is a sense of community. The men, women, and children in this picture may well have joined in the hymn "We Gather Together" with the same enthusiasm they brought to their preparations for a hearty Thanksgiving dinner.

Tureen. French (Strasbourg), ca. 1750. Tin-glazed earthenware.

Thanksgiving Turkey. Anna Mary Robertson Moses, American, 1860–1961. Tempera and oil on Masonite, 1943.

YANKEE DOODLE

This high-spirited song has been popular in America since colonial days, but the tune is much older. Harvesters in Holland sang the nonsense words "Yanker dudel doodle down," as did mothers and nurses to small children in England in Shakespeare's time. The words known in the United States are said to have been written by a British army surgeon to make fun of the untrained colonial troops during the French and Indian War in 1755. ("Macaroni" was the English term for young dandies who dressed in odd foreign styles.) But the Continental soldiers who fought in the American Revolution more than twenty years later liked "Yankee Doodle" so much that it was soon sung and played in every patriot camp, and soldiers even whistled the tune in battle. The army officer on his prancing steed on the painted chest from Pennsylvania looks as dashing as "Captain Washington" on his "slapping stallion." The buoyant song sounds best when accompanied by the shrill tones of the fife and the rhythmic beating of a drum.

Snare drum. American, 19th century. Wood, skin, and rope.

Brisk march

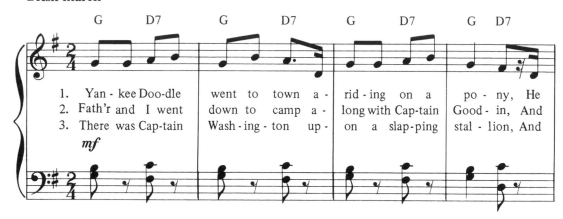

1. Yan-kee Doo-dle went to town a-rid-ing on a po-ny, He
2. Fath'r and I went down to camp a-long with Cap-tain Good-in, And
3. There was Cap-tain Wash-ing-ton up-on a slap-ping stal-lion, And

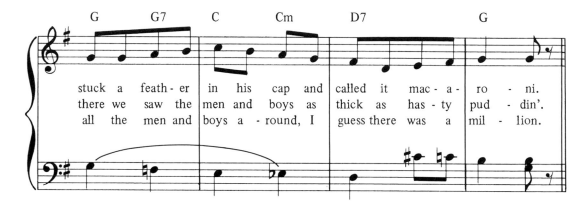

stuck a feath-er in his cap and called it mac-a-ro-ni.
there we saw the men and boys as thick as has-ty pud-din'.
all the men and boys a-round, I guess there was a mil-lion.

Chorus

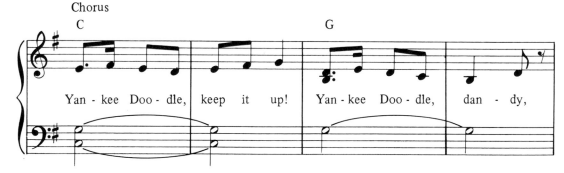

Yan-kee Doo-dle, keep it up! Yan-kee Doo-dle, dan-dy,

Mind the mu-sic and the step And with the girls be hand-y.

Detail of a dower chest. American (Berks County, Pennsylvania), ca. 1780. Painted yellow pine and tulip poplar.

CREDITS

INDEX OF FIRST LINES

GUITAR CHORD DIAGRAMS

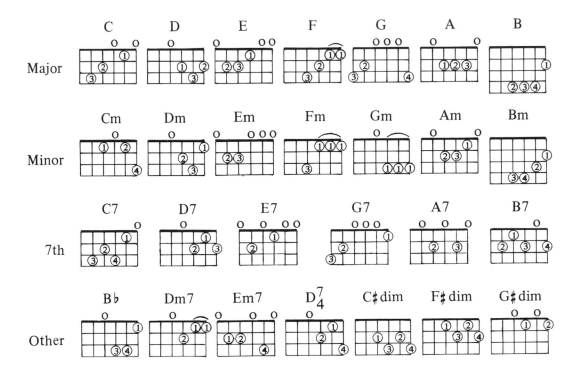

	C	D	E	F	G	A	B
Major							

	Cm	Dm	Em	Fm	Gm	Am	Bm
Minor							

	C7	D7	E7	G7	A7	B7
7th						

	B♭	Dm7	Em7	D$\frac{7}{4}$	C♯dim	F♯dim	G♯dim
Other